CW01637309

How to access your online resources

Kaplan Financial students will have a MyKaplan account and these extra resources will be available to you online. You do not need to register again, as this process was completed when you enrolled. If you are having problems accessing online materials, please ask your course administrator.

If you are not studying with Kaplan and did not purchase your book via a Kaplan website, to unlock your extra online resources please go to **www.mykaplan.co.uk/add-online-resources** (even if you have set up an account and registered books previously). You will then need to enter the ISBN number (on the title page and back cover) and the unique pass key number contained in the scratch panel below to gain access.

You will also be required to enter additional information during this process to set up or confirm your account details.

If you purchased through the Kaplan Publishing website you will automatically receive an e-mail invitation to register your details and gain access to your content. If you do not receive the e-mail or book content, please contact Kaplan Publishing.

This code can only be used once for the registration of this book online. This registration and your online content will expire when the examinations covered by this book have taken place. Please allow one hour from the time you submit your book details for us to process your request.

Please scratch the film to access your unique code.

Please be aware that this code is case-sensitive and you will need to include the dashes within the passcode, but not when entering the ISBN.

KAPLAN PUBLISHING

CIMA's CGMA® 2019 Professional Examinations

CIMA's CGMA Operational Level

Subject P1

Management Accounting

EXAM PRACTICE KIT

CIMA™

KAPLAN PUBLISHING

Published by: Kaplan Publishing UK

Unit 2 The Business Centre, Molly Millars Lane, Wokingham, Berkshire RG41 2QZ

Acknowledgements

We are grateful to the CIMA for permission to reproduce past examination questions. The answers to CIMA Exams have been prepared by Kaplan Publishing, except in the case of the CIMA November 2010 and subsequent CIMA Exam answers where the official CIMA answers have been reproduced. Questions from past live assessments have been included by kind permission of CIMA,

Notice

The text in this material and any others made available by any Kaplan Group company does not amount to advice on a particular matter and should not be taken as such. No reliance should be placed on the content as the basis for any investment or other decision or in connection with any advice given to third parties. Please consult your appropriate professional adviser as necessary.

Kaplan Publishing Limited and all other Kaplan group companies expressly disclaim all liability to any person in respect of any losses or other claims, whether direct, indirect, incidental, consequential or otherwise arising in relation to the use of such materials.

Kaplan is not responsible for the content of external websites. The inclusion of a link to a third party website in this text should not be taken as an endorsement.

Kaplan Publishing's learning materials are designed to help students succeed in their examinations. In certain circumstances, CIMA can make post-exam adjustment to a student's mark or grade to reflect adverse circumstances which may have disadvantaged a student's ability to take an exam or demonstrate their normal level of attainment (see CIMA's Special Consideration policy). However, it should be noted that students will not be eligible for special consideration by CIMA if preparation for or performance in a CIMA exam is affected by any failure by their tuition provider to prepare them properly for the exam for any reason including, but not limited to, staff shortages, building work or a lack of facilities etc.

Similarly, CIMA will not accept applications for special consideration on any of the following grounds:

- failure by a tuition provider to cover the whole syllabus
- failure by the student to cover the whole syllabus, for instance as a result of joining a course part way through
- failure by the student to prepare adequately for the exam, or to use the correct pre-seen material
- errors in the Kaplan Official Study Text, including sample (practice) questions or any other Kaplan content or
- errors in any other study materials (from any other tuition provider or publisher).

British Library Cataloguing in Publication Data

A catalogue record for this book is available from the British Library.

ISBN: 978-1-83735-102-2

Printed and bound in Great Britain

CONTENTS

Section

Quality and accuracy are of the utmost importance to us so if you spot an error in any of our products, please send an email to mykaplanreporting@kaplan.com with full details.

Our Quality Co-ordinator will work with our technical team to verify the error and take action to ensure it is corrected in future editions.

INDEX TO QUESTIONS AND ANSWERS

OBJECTIVE TEST QUESTIONS

EXAM TECHNIQUES

COMPUTER-BASED ASSESSMENT

Golden rules

1 Make sure you have completed the compulsory 15-minute tutorial before you start the test. This tutorial is available through the AICPA & CIMA website and focusses on the functionality of the exam. You cannot speak to the invigilator once you have started.

2 These exam practice kits give you plenty of exam style questions to practise so make sure you use them to fully prepare.

3 Attempt all questions, there is no negative marking.

4 Double check your answer before you put in the final answer although you can change your response as many times as you like.

5 Not all questions will be multiple choice questions (MCQs) – you may have to fill in missing words or figures.

6 Identify the easy questions first and get some points on the board to build up your confidence.

7 Attempt 'wordy' questions first as these may be quicker than the computation style questions. This will relieve some of the time pressure you will be under during the exam.

8 If you don't know the answer, flag the question and attempt it later. In your final review before the end of the exam try a process of elimination.

9 Work out your answer on the whiteboard provided first if it is easier for you. There is also an onscreen 'scratch pad' on which you can make notes. You are not allowed to take pens, pencils, rulers, pencil cases, phones, paper or notes into the testing room.

SYLLABUS GUIDANCE, LEARNING OBJECTIVES AND VERBS

A CIMA's CGMA® 2019 PROFESSIONAL QUALIFICATION

Details regarding the content of CIMA's CGMA 2019 Professional Qualification can be located within the CGMA 2019 Professional Qualification syllabus document.

You can use the following diagram showing the whole structure of your qualification to help you keep track of your progress. Make sure you seek appropriate advice if you are unsure about your progression through the qualification.

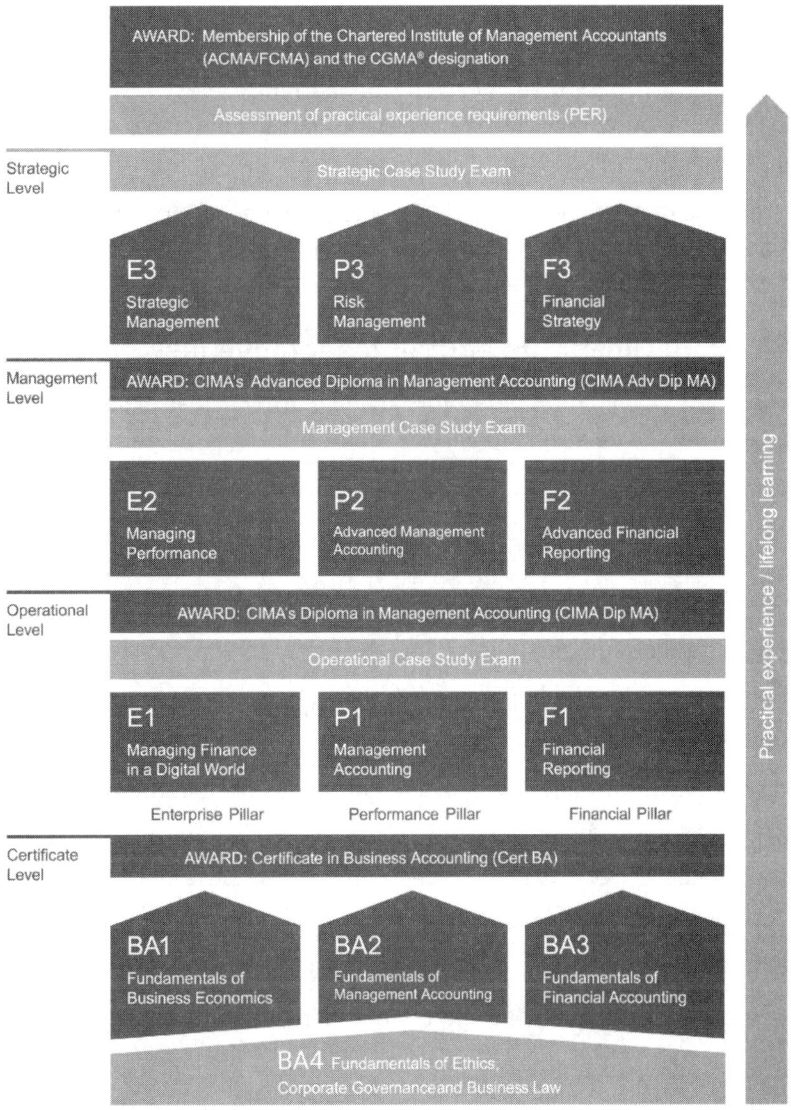

Reproduced with CIMA's permission

B STUDY WEIGHTINGS

A percentage weighting is shown against each exam content area in CIMA's CGMA® Exam Blueprints. This is intended as a guide to the proportion of study time each topic requires.

All component learning outcomes will be tested.

The weightings do not specify the number of marks that will be allocated to topics in the examination.

C LEARNING OUTCOMES

Each subject within the qualification is divided into a number of broad syllabus topics. The topics contain one or more lead learning outcomes, related component learning outcomes and indicative knowledge content.

A learning outcome has two main purposes:

1 to define the skill or ability that a well-prepared candidate should be able to exhibit in the examination

2 to demonstrate the approach likely to be taken by examiners in examination questions.

The learning outcomes are part of a hierarchy of learning objectives. The verbs used at the beginning of each learning outcome relate to a specific learning objective, e.g., Evaluate alternative approaches to budgeting.

The verb 'evaluate' indicates a high-level learning objective. As learning objectives are hierarchical, it is expected that at this level students will have knowledge of different budgeting systems and methodologies and be able to apply them.

CIMA's CGMA Exam Blueprints and representative task statements

CIMA has also published examination blueprints giving learners clear expectations regarding what is expected of them. This can be accessed via the AICPA & CIMA website.

The blueprint is structured as follows:

- Exam content sections (reflecting the syllabus document)
- Lead and component outcomes (reflecting the syllabus document)
- Representative task statements.

A representative task statement is a plain English description of what a CGMA® qualified finance professional should know and be able to do.

The content and skill level determine the language and verbs used in the representative task.

CIMA will test up to the level of the task statement in the Objective Test (an Objective Test question on a particular topic could be set at a lower level than the task statement in the blueprint).

The format of the Objective Test blueprints follows that of the published syllabus for the 2019 Professional Qualification.

Weightings for content sections are also included in the individual subject blueprints.

A list of the learning objectives and the verbs that appear in the syllabus learning outcomes and examinations follows and these will help you to understand the depth and breadth required for a topic and the skill level the topic relates to.

CIMA's verb hierarchy

Skill level	Verbs used	Definition
Level 5 Evaluation How you are expected to use your learning to evaluate, make decisions or recommendations	Advise	Counsel, inform or notify
	Assess	Evaluate or estimate the nature, ability or quality of
	Evaluate	Appraise or assess the value of
	Recommend	Propose a course of action
	Review	Assess and evaluate in order, to change if necessary
Level 4 Analysis How you are expected to analyse the detail of what you have learned	Align	Arrange in an orderly way
	Analyse	Examine in detail the structure of
	Communicate	Share or exchange information
	Compare and contrast	Show the similarities and/or differences between
	Develop	Grow and expand a concept
	Discuss	Examine in detail by argument
	Examine	Inspect thoroughly
	Interpret	Translate into intelligible or familiar terms
	Monitor	Observe and check the progress of
	Prioritise	Place in order of priority or sequence for action
	Produce	Create or bring into existence
Level 3 Application How you are expected to apply your knowledge	Apply	Put to practical use
	Calculate	Ascertain or reckon mathematically
	Conduct	Organise and carry out
	Demonstrate	Prove with certainty or exhibit by practical means
	Prepare	Make or get ready for use
	Reconcile	Make or prove consistent/compatible
Level 2 Comprehension What you are expected to understand	Describe	Communicate the key features of
	Distinguish	Highlight the differences between
	Explain	Make clear or intelligible/state the meaning or purpose of
	Identify	Recognise, establish or select after consideration
	Illustrate	Use an example to describe or explain something
Level 1 Knowledge What you are expected to know	List	Make a list of
	State	Express, fully or clearly, the details/facts of
	Define	Give the exact meaning of
	Outline	Give a summary of

D OBJECTIVE TEST

Objective Test

Objective Test questions require you to choose or provide a response to a question whose correct answer is predetermined.

The most common types of Objective Test question you will see are:

- Multiple choice, where you have to choose the correct answer(s) from a list of possible answers. This could either be numbers or text.
- Multiple response, for example, choosing two correct answers from a list of eight possible answers. This could either be numbers or text.
- Fill in the blank, where you fill in your answer within the provided space.
- Drag and drop, for example, matching a technical term with the correct definition.
- Hot spots, where you select an answer by clicking on graphs/diagrams.

Guidance on CIMA's on-screen calculator

As part of the CGMA Objective Test software, candidates are now provided with a calculator. This calculator is on-screen and is available for the duration of the assessment. The calculator is available in each of the Objective Tests and is accessed by clicking the calculator button in the top left hand corner of the screen at any time during the assessment. Candidates are permitted to utilise personal calculators as long as they are an approved CIMA model. CIMA approved model list can be found on the AICPA & CIMA website.

All candidates must complete a 15-minute exam tutorial before the assessment begins and will have the opportunity to familiarise themselves with the calculator and practise using it. The exam tutorial is also available online via the AICPA & CIMA website. Candidates can use their own calculators providing it is included in CIMA's authorised calculator listing.

Fundamentals of Objective Tests

The Objective Tests are 90-minute assessments comprising 60 compulsory questions, with one or more parts. There will be no choice and all questions should be attempted. All elements of a question must be answered correctly for the question to be marked correctly. All questions are equally weighted.

APPROACH TO REVISION

Stage 1: Assess areas of strengths and weaknesses

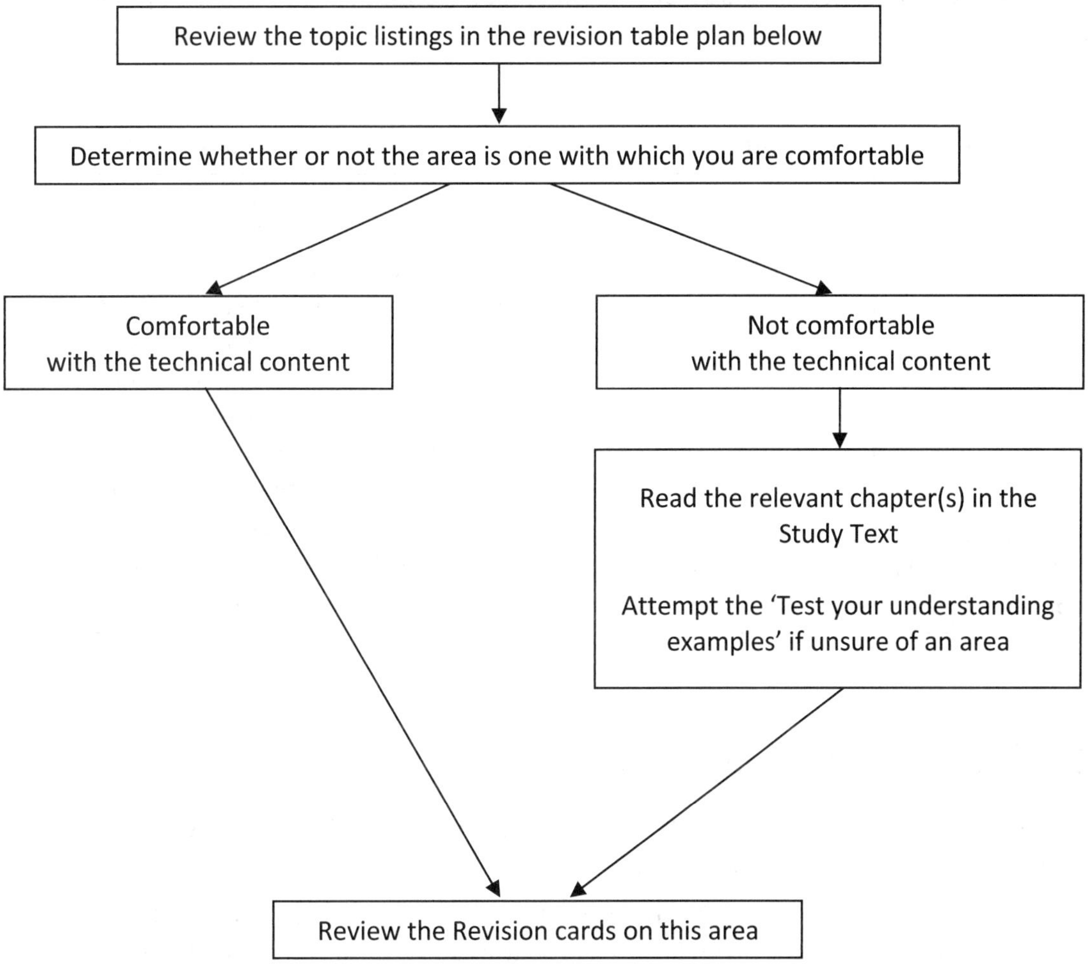

Stage 2: Question practice

Follow the order of revision of topics as recommended in the revision table plan below and attempt the questions in the order suggested.

Try to avoid referring to textbooks and notes and the model answer until you have completed your attempt.

Try to answer the question in the allotted time.

Review your attempt with the model answer and assess how much of the answer you achieved in the allocated exam time.

Comfortable with question attempt

↓

Only revisit when comfortable with questions on all topic areas

Not comfortable with question attempts

↓

Focus on these areas by:

- Reworking 'Test your understanding examples' in the Study Text
- Revisiting the technical content from the Revision cards
- Working any remaining questions on that area in the Exam Practice Kit
- Reattempting an exam standard question in that area, on a timed, closed book basis

Stage 3: Final pre-exam revision

We recommend that you **attempt at least one ninety minute mock examination** containing a set of previously unseen exam standard questions.

It is important that you get a feel for the breadth of coverage of a real exam without advanced knowledge of the topic areas covered – just as you will expect to see on the real exam day.

Ideally a mock examination offered by your tuition provider should be sat in timed, closed book, real exam conditions.

CGMA SYLLABUS GRIDS

P1: Management Accounting

What the finance function does

Content weighting

Content area		Weighting
A	Cost accounting for decision and control	30%
B	Budgeting and budgetary control	25%
C	Short-term commercial decision-making	30%
D	Risk and uncertainty in the short term	15%
		100%

P1A: Cost accounting for decision and control

This section is about understanding why costing is done and what it is used for. It introduces candidates to the basic building blocks of costing and how to apply them in the costing methods and techniques organisations use. In a fast-changing digital world this understanding is critical and can enable candidates to develop their own ways of calculating costs when existing methods are no longer appropriate. Digital costing is introduced in this section.

Lead outcome	Component outcome	Topics to be covered	Explanatory notes
1. Distinguish between the different rationales for costing.	a. Define costing b. Distinguish between the rationales for costing	• Inventory valuation • Profit reporting • Cost management and transformation • Decision-making	This seeks to address the following pertinent questions: What are reasons for calculating costs? What types of costs are appropriate for a particular purpose and why?
2. Apply the main costing concepts to organisations and cost objects.	a. Explain the main costing concepts b. Apply costing concepts to different organisations and cost objects	• Cost elements • Costs structure • Cost behaviour • Cost drivers • Costing applied to different types of organisations • Costing applied to digital cost objects	Examine the basic building blocks of costing and how they apply to different types of organisations and operating contexts (e.g., manufacturing and service sectors). How has the digital world affected the nature of these building blocks of costing?
3. Apply costing methods to determine the costs for different purposes.	Apply the following: a. Cost accumulation, allocation, apportionment and absorption b. Standard costing c. Variance analysis (without mix and yield variance) d. Activity based costing e. Digital costing f. Quality costing g. Environmental costing	• Trace, classify and allocate costs • Marginal costing • Absorption costing • Price and rate variances • Usage and efficiency variances • Interpretation of variances • Product and service costing using ABC • Advantages of ABC over other costing systems • Features of digital costing	Investigate how costs are traced, classified, accumulated, allocated, apportioned and absorbed to arrive at the costs of a product, service or other cost object. Calculate the costs of products or services using various costing methods. Determine which costing methods are appropriate and why?

P1B: Budgeting and budgetary control

Taken together, budgeting and budgetary control is one way the finance function enables and shapes how organisations create and preserve value. This section examines the various reasons organisations prepare and use budgets, how the budgets are prepared, the types and sources of data, the technologies used to improve the quality of budgets, how budgets are implemented and the impact on the people who work with the organisation.

Lead outcome	Component outcome	Topics to be covered	Explanatory notes
1. Distinguish between the different rationales for budgeting.	a. Explain the role of budgets. b. Distinguish between the different rationales for budgeting.	• Planning • Communication • Coordination • Motivation • Control	Why do organisations prepare budgets? In what ways are the different rationales for preparing budgets compatible with each other? How do organisations get the most out the budgeting process?
2. Prepare budgets.	a. Explain forecasting and its relationship with budgeting. b. Prepare master budgets. c. Conduct what-if analysis in budgeting. d. Describe the technologies available for improving budgeting.	• Time series and trend analysis to forecast sales volumes • Components of master budgets and their interaction with each other • Limiting factors • Stress testing budgets • Big data analytics and budgets • Alternative approaches to budgeting	What is the process by which budgets are prepared? What types of budgets are required by organisations? What data do they use and where do they get the data from? How are those budgets prepared and presented? What technologies are available for improving the quality of the budgets?
3. Discuss budgetary control.	Discuss: a. The concept of budgetary control b. Human dimensions of budgeting	• Feedback and feedforward control • Flexed budgets • Target setting and motivation • Controllable and uncontrollable outcomes • Dysfunctional behaviours in budgeting • Ethical considerations in budgeting	What is budgetary control? Describe and discuss how and why the budgetary control system provides feedback and feedforward to the organisation. What are the behavioural impacts of budgetary control and how are they managed?

P1C: Short-term commercial decision-making

Organisations cannot foresee every opportunity that might arise during their operations, so they need mechanisms by which to identify and take advantage of these opportunities as they arise. The primary objective of this section is to guide candidates in how to do this in the short term through effective decision-making. The finance function supports such decisions (e.g., pricing and product choice) using techniques such as relevant revenue and cost analysis and break- even analysis. Candidates are introduced to these techniques and the concepts that underpin the techniques. They are expected to be able to apply the techniques to support short-term decision-making.

Lead outcome	Component outcome	Topics to be covered	Explanatory notes
1. Describe the main types of short-term decisions made by organisations.	a. Describe pricing and revenue maximising decisions. b. Describe product decisions.	• Marginal and full cost recovery for pricing decisions • Differences in pricing and revenue maximisation for the short term and long term • Product mix	Describe the types of short-term decisions organisations make and the circumstances that give rise to them. What do these short-term decisions seek to achieve? How important are they to performance of organisations? The emphasis is on both revenue and costs.
2. Explain the underlying concepts used for short-term decision-making.	a. Explain the objectives of decision-making. b. Explain the underlying concepts of short-term decision-making.	• Implications of commercial decision-making in the short term • Relevant revenues • Relevant costs • Difference with profit reporting	What are the objectives and underlying concepts that are used to guide short-term decision-making and why? Distinguish between those concepts of revenue, costs and information from other concepts.
3. Apply appropriate techniques to support short-term decisions.	Apply the following to support short-term decision-making: a. Relevant cost analysis b. Break-even analysis c. Product mix decisions with constraints d. Data and technology	• Make or buy decisions • Discontinuation decisions • Multi-product break-even analysis • Use of data and technology to analyse product mix decisions • Ethical considerations in short-term decision-making	Use data (financial and non-financial) and the appropriate concepts and techniques to support decision-making to achieve organisational objectives of value creation and preservation.

P1D: Risk and uncertainty in the short term

Budgets and decisions focus on the future. This introduces uncertainties and risks that need to be identified, assessed and managed. The aim of this section is to help candidates identify, assess and manage the risks and uncertainties associated with the short term.

Lead outcome	Component outcome	Topics to be covered	Explanatory notes
1. Apply basic risk management tools in the short term.	a. Explain nature of risk and uncertainty in short term. b. Apply basic sensitivity analysis to budgeting and short-term decision-making.	• Stress testing • Sensitivity and what-if analysis • Probability distributions • Decision trees	What types of risks and uncertainties do organisations face when preparing and implementing budgets and when making short-term decisions? How are those risks and uncertainties identified, assessed and managed?

Information concerning formulae and tables will be provided via the CIMA website, www.aicpa-cima.com

Section 1

OBJECTIVE TEST QUESTIONS

COST ACCOUNTING FOR DECISION AND CONTROL

RATIONALES FOR COSTING

1 **Which of the following is NOT one of the main purposes of management accounting?**

A Planning

B Reporting

C Decision Making

D Controlling

2 **Do the comments below relate to management or financial accounting? (Tick the correct system)**

	Management accounting	**Financial accounting**
Uses only historical data		
Is carried out at the discretion of management		
Uses non-financial information		
Aids planning within the organisation		

3 **Which TWO of the following would normally be carried out by strategic level management?**

	Strategic?
Making day-to-day decisions about the running of a department	
Defining the objectives of the company	
Deciding in which markets to operate	
Deciding about how to compete within their chosen markets	
Inventory control	

4 **Direct costs are:**

A costs which can be identified with a cost centre but not identified to a single cost unit

B costs which can be economically identified with a single cost unit

C costs which can be identified with a single cost unit, but it is not economic to do so

D costs incurred as a direct result of a particular decision

5 Which of the following descriptions best suits the graph below?

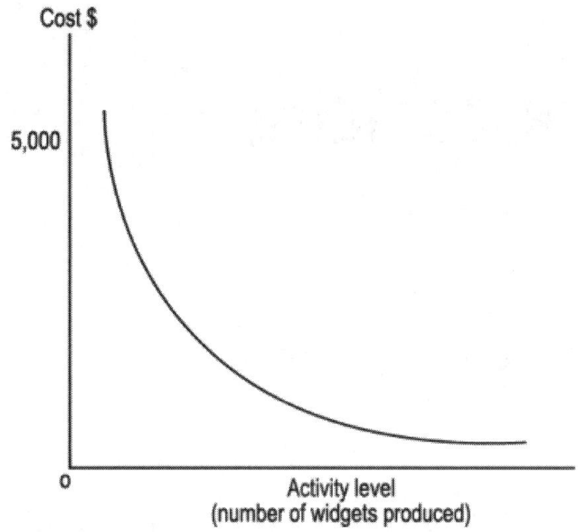

A Total fixed costs

B Total variable costs

C Variable cost per unit

D Fixed cost per unit

6 Which of the following would be classified as direct labour?

A An HR manager in a company servicing cars

B Builder's wages in a construction company

C General manager's salary in a DIY shop

D Maintenance manager in a company producing cameras

7 XYZ Ltd is preparing the production budget for the next period. The total costs of production are a semi-variable cost. The following cost information has been collected in connection with production:

Volume (units)	Cost
4,500	$29,000
6,500	$33,000

What are the estimated total production costs for a production volume of 5,750 units?

A $29,200

B $30,000

C $31,500

D $32,500

8 The budgeted total costs for two levels of output are as shown below:

Output	25,000 units	40,000 units
Total cost	$143,500	$194,000

Within this range of output, it is known that the variable cost per unit is constant but fixed costs rise by $10,000 when output exceeds 35,000 units.

What are the total fixed costs for a budgeted output of 36,000 units?

9 A company is preparing its maintenance budget. The number of machine hours and maintenance costs for the past six months have been as follows:

Month	**Machine hours**	**$**
1	10,364	35,319
2	12,212	39,477
3	8,631	31,420
4	9,460	33,285
5	8,480	31,080
6	10,126	34,784

The budget cost allowance for an activity level of 9,340 machine hours, before any adjustment for price changes, is nearest to:

A $21,000

B $30,200

C $33,000

D $34,000

10 A company is estimating its costs based on past information. The total costs incurred by the company at different levels of output were as follows:

Output (units)	**Total costs** ($)
160,000	2,420,000
185,000	2,775,000
190,000	2,840,000

The company uses the high-low method to separate total costs into their fixed and variable elements. Ignore inflation. The company has now established that there is a stepped increase in fixed costs of $30,000 when output reaches 180,000 units.

What is the estimate of total costs for an output of 175,000 units?

A $2,645,000

B $2,275,000

C $2,615,000

D $2,630,000

11 The CGMA Cost Transformation Model has been developed to provide a framework to help businesses achieve and maintain their cost-competitiveness.

The Finance Director of H Ltd is concerned that production overhead costs are spiralling out of control. It current operates a traditional absorption costing system using a factory-wide absorption rate per machine hour but is considering changing to an activity-based costing system in an attempt to allocate overheads more fairly.

Which area of the Cost Transformation Model does this action best represent?

A Maximising value from new products

B Managing the risks that come from a cost conscious culture

C Considering the environmental impact of products

D Understanding cost drivers

TRADITIONAL COSTING

12 A business reported a marginal costing profit of $45,000 last period. Its inventory values for the period were as follows:

	$
Opening inventory	16,000
Closing inventory	20,800

If the business had used absorption costing, the inventory values would have been as follows:

	$
Opening inventory	28,000
Closing inventory	36,400

What would have been the reported profit using absorption costing?

A $41,400

B $48,600

C $57,000

D $60,600

13 A company has a budget to produce 5,000 units of Product B in December. The budget for December shows that, for Product B, the opening inventory will be 400 units and the closing inventory will be 900 units. The monthly budgeted production cost data for Product B for December is as follows:

Variable direct costs per unit	$6.00
Variable production overhead costs per unit	$3.50
Total fixed production overhead costs	$29,500

The company absorbs overheads on the basis of the budgeted number of units produced.

The budgeted profit for Product B for December, using absorption costing, is:

A $2,950 lower than it would be using marginal costing

B $2,950 greater than it would be using marginal costing

C $4,700 lower than it would be using marginal costing

D $4,700 greater than it would be using marginal costing

14 A company operates an absorption costing system. The budgeted fixed production overheads for the company for the latest year were $330,000 and budgeted output was 220,000 units. At the end of the company's financial year the total of the fixed production overheads debited to the fixed production overhead control account was $260,000 and the actual output achieved was 200,000 units.

The under/over absorption of overheads was:

A $40,000 over absorbed

B $40,000 under absorbed

C $70,000 over absorbed

D $70,000 under absorbed

15 A business manufactures a single product which sells for $45 per unit. The budgeted data for the latest period are as follows:

Production and sales volume	2,000 units
	$
Material cost	13,500
Direct labour cost	11,800
Production overhead	32,400
Non-production overhead	21,900

Actual production volume and costs were as budgeted for the period but the actual sales volume achieved was 1,800 units. There was no inventory at the beginning of the period.

The profit for the period using absorption costing is $_____

16 Which of the following statements are correct (tick all that apply)?

		Correct?
(i)	A cost driver is any factor that causes a change in the cost of an activity.	
(ii)	For long-term variable overhead costs, the cost driver will be the volume of activity.	
(iii)	Traditional absorption costing tends to under-allocate overhead costs to low-volume products.	

17 H Ltd manufactures a single product which sells for $120 per unit. The budgeted data for the latest period are as follows:

Production and sales volume	5,000 units
	$
Material cost	126,500
Direct labour cost	76,800
Production overhead	68,000
Non-production overhead	23,900

Actual production volume and costs were as budgeted for the period but the actual sales volume achieved was 4,100 units. There was no inventory at the beginning of the period.

The profit for the period using marginal costing is $_____

18 T uses a standard labour hour rate to charge its overheads to its clients' work. During the last annual reporting period production overheads were under-absorbed by $19,250. The anticipated standard labour hours for the period were 38,000 hours while the standard hours actually charged to clients were 38,500. The actual production overheads incurred in the period were $481,250.

The budgeted production overheads for the period were:

A $456,000

B $462,000

C $475,000

D $498,000

19 WTD Ltd produces a single product. The management currently uses marginal costing but is considering using absorption costing in the future.

The budgeted fixed production overheads for the period are $500,000. The budgeted output for the period is 2,000 units. There were 800 units of opening inventory at the beginning of the period and 500 units of closing inventory at the end of the period.

If absorption costing principles were applied, the profit for the period compared to the marginal costing profit would be:

A $75,000 higher

B $75,000 lower

C $125,000 higher

D $125,000 lower

20 **Overheads will ALWAYS be over-absorbed when:**

A actual output is higher than budgeted output

B actual overheads incurred are higher than the amount absorbed

C actual overheads incurred are lower than the amount absorbed

D budgeted overheads are lower than the overheads absorbed

21 X Ltd has two production departments, Assembly and Finishing, and two service departments, Stores and Maintenance.

A junior member of the finance department has allocated, apportioned and reapportioned the fixed production overheads for each department as follows:

	Assembly	**Finishing**	**Stores**	**Maintenance**	**Total**
Budgeted overhead	100,000	150,000	50,000	40,000	340,000
Reapportion maintenance	16,000	18,000	6,000	(40,000)	–
			56,000		
Reapportion stores	33,600	22,400	(56,000)		–
Total overhead	149,600	190,400			340,000

The budgeted output for the year was 100,000 units.

At the end of the year after apportioning the service department overheads, the total fixed production overheads debited to the Assembly department's fixed production overhead control account were $180,000.

The actual output achieved was 120,000 units.

The under-/over-absorption of fixed production overheads for the Assembly department is $_______

22 Summary results for Y Ltd for March are shown below:

	$000	**Units**
Sales revenue	820	
Variable production costs	300	
Variable selling costs	105	
Fixed production costs	180	
Fixed selling costs	110	
Production in March		1,000
Opening inventory		0
Closing inventory		150

Using marginal costing, the profit for March was:

A $170,000

B $185,750

C $197,000

D $229,250

23 GH produces three models of speedboat for sale to the retail market. GH currently operates a standard absorption costing system. Budgeting information for next year is given below:

Model of speedboat	**Superior**	**Deluxe**	**Ultra**	**Total**
	$000	$000	$000	$000
Sales	54,000	86,400	102,000	242,400
Direct material	17,600	27,400	40,200	85,200
Direct labour	10,700	13,400	16,600	40,700
Production overhead				69,600
Gross profit				46,900

	Superior	**Deluxe**	**Ultra**
Production/sales (number of boats)	1,000	1,200	800
Machine hours per boat	100	200	300

The production overhead cost is absorbed using a machine hour rate.

The total gross profit for the Deluxe speedboat using absorption costing is $______

24 **Which ONE of the following statements regarding overheads is correct?**

A allocation is where the overhead related to more than one production and/or service cost centre is shared between these cost centres

B with traditional absorption costing, overheads will always be absorbed by number of units produced, machine hours worked or labour hours worked

C overhead absorption rates are typically calculated at the end of the period

D absorption costing may result in manipulation of profits

25 **Which TWO of the following are advantages of marginal costing?**

A it ensures that inventories are valued in accordance with financial reporting standards

B it simplifies the process of cost accounting

C it is the most appropriate system for long-term decision-making

D it avoids the arbitrary apportionment of overheads

ACTIVITY BASED COSTING

26 A food-processing company operates an activity based costing (ABC) system. **Determine whether the following would be classified as a facility- or product-sustaining activity (place a tick in the box corresponding to any that would apply)?**

		Facility-sustaining	**Product-sustaining**
(i)	General staff administration		
(ii)	Plant management		
(iii)	Technical support for individual products and services		
(iv)	Updating of product specification database		
(v)	Property management		

27 P operates an activity based costing (ABC) system to attribute its overhead costs to cost objects.

In its budget for the year ending 31 August 20X6, the company expected to place a total of 2,895 purchase orders at a total cost of $110,010. This activity and its related costs were budgeted to occur at a constant rate throughout the budget year, which is divided into 13 four-week periods.

During the four-week period ended 30 June 20X6, a total of 210 purchase orders were placed at a cost of $7,650.

The over-recovery of these costs for the four-week period was:

A $330

B $350

C $370

D $390

28 DRP has recently introduced an Activity Based Costing system. It manufactures three products:

	Product D	**Product R**	**Product P**
Budgeted annual production (units)	100,000	100,000	50,000
Batch size (units)	100	50	25
Machine set-ups per batch	3	4	6
Purchase orders per batch	2	1	1
Processing time per unit (minutes)	2	3	3
Budgeted number of batches	1,000	2,000	2,000

Three cost pools have been identified. Their budgeted costs for 20X4 are as follows:

Machine set-up costs $150,000

Purchasing of materials $70,000

Processing $80,000

The cost per unit attributed to Product R for machine set ups is $_____

29 K Ltd makes three products and uses an activity based costing system. The stores receiving costs, which are driven by the number of component deliveries, make up $6,840 of the total production overhead cost.

Driver analysis for K Ltd revealed the following information:

Product	**X**	**Y**	**Z**
Budgeted production (units)	1,000	1,200	800
Number of component deliveries	500	600	800
Number of issues from stores	4,000	5,000	7,000

The total cost attributed to Product Y for component deliveries using the proposed activity based costing system is $_______

30 HZ makes three products and is considering changing to an activity based costing system. The quality inspection costs make up $14,140 of the total production overhead cost.

Driver analysis for HZ revealed the following information:

Product	**A**	**B**	**C**
Budgeted production	1,000	1,200	800
Production units per production run	5	4	2
Quality inspections per production run	10	20	30

The total cost attributed to Product C for quality inspections using an activity based costing system is $_______

31 **Which of the following explains why an activity based costing system may produce more accurate product costs than a traditional absorption costing system?**

Cost	**Advantage?**
Better cost control is possible	
Arbitrary allocations of costs are avoided	
Better product pricing is possible	
The choice of cost drivers is easy	
Can be applied to service companies	

32 An accountancy firm provides three main services to its customers and uses activity based costing. As part of each service, customer files will be regularly reviewed. The review costs are allocated to each service according to the average number of reviews per service.

The cost driver for reviews is:

A a duration driver

B a transaction driver

C a facility driver

D an intensity driver

33 LMN has recently introduced an Activity Based Costing system. It manufactures three products:

	Product L	**Product M**	**Product N**
Budgeted annual production (units)	300,000	300,000	150,000
Batch size (units)	1,000	2,000	2,000
Machine set-ups per batch	4	2	5
Purchase orders per batch	2	3	2
Processing time per unit (minutes)	4	6	6

Three cost pools have been identified. Their budgeted costs for the year are as follows:

Machine set-up costs $250,000

Purchasing of materials $105,000

Processing $156,000

The cost per unit attributed to Product L for processing time is $_____

OTHER ELEMENTS OF COSTING

34 Company B uses a throughput accounting system. The details of product X per unit are as follows:

Selling price	$50
Material cost	$16
Conversion costs	$20
Time on bottleneck resource	8 minutes

The return per hour for product X is:

A $105

B $225

C $255

D $375

35 A company can produce many types of product but is currently restricted by the number of labour hours available on a particular machine. At present this limitation is set at 12,000 hours per annum. One type of product requires materials costing $5 which are then converted to a final product that sells for $12. Each unit of this product takes 45 minutes to produce on the machine. The conversion costs for the factory are estimated to be $144,000 per annum.

The throughput accounting ratio for this product is _____ (answer to three decimal places).

36 **What is defined as 'an activity within an organisation which has a lower capacity than preceding or subsequent activities, thereby limiting throughput'?**

A Bottleneck

B Constraint

C Limiting factor

D Restraint

37 A company produces two products, S and T, which pass through two production processes, X and Y. The time taken to make each product in each process is:

	Product S	**Product T**
Process X	5 mins	7.5 mins
Process Y	18 mins	12 mins

The company operates a 15-hour day and has an average downtime each day of:

Process X	1.5 hours
Process Y	1.0 hours

Sales demand restricts the output of S and T to 50 and 80 units a day respectively.

Process ___ (enter X or Y) is the bottleneck process.

38 The following data relate to a manufacturing company. At the beginning of August there was no inventory. During August 2,000 units of Product X were produced, but only 1,750 units were sold. The financial data for Product X for August were as follows:

	$
Materials	40,000
Labour	12,600
Variable production overheads	9,400
Fixed production overheads	22,500
Variable selling costs	6,000
Fixed selling costs	19,300
Total costs for X for August	109,800

The value of inventory of X at 31 August using a throughput accounting approach is $_______

39 A business manufactures a single product which sells for $45 per unit. The budgeted data for the latest period are as follows:

Production and sales volume	**2,000 units**
	$
Material cost	13,500
Direct labour cost	11,800
Production overhead	32,400
Non-production overhead	21,900

Actual production volume and costs were as budgeted for the period but the actual sales volume achieved was 1,800 units. There was no inventory at the beginning of the period.

The profit for the period using throughput accounting is $_____

40 A manufacturing company recorded the following costs in October for Product X:

	$
Direct materials	20,000
Direct labour	6,300
Variable production overhead	4,700
Fixed production overhead	19,750
Variable selling costs	4,500
Fixed distribution costs	16,800
Total costs incurred for Product X	72,050

During October 4,000 units of Product X were produced but only 3,600 units were sold. At the beginning of October there was no inventory.

The value of the inventory of Product X at the end of October using throughput accounting was:

A $630

B $1,080

C $1,100

D $2,000

41 A chemicals manufacturer is assessing the environmental costs associated with the waste that the business releases into the environment.

Which of the following costs related to the company's waste would be classified as an environmental prevention cost?

A Fines for non-compliance with environmental regulations

B The harm done to wildlife due to toxic waste spills

C Cost of installing new filters and treatment processes to reduce toxicity of waste

D Reputational damage due to negative publicity from environmental groups

42 **Which of the following statements regarding digital products is NOT true?**

A The high marginal cost of digital products makes them difficult to price

B The life span of digital products can vary greatly

C There are often recurring costs for digital products

D Determining cost drivers for digital products can be very difficult

43 A company with audio expertise has had great success in selling physical testing equipment to amateurs who want to personalise their home listening experience. It is now considering providing the testing software through a downloadable mobile application.

Consider whether the following are likely to be higher or lower for the mobile phone application than for the existing physical equipment:

	Higher	**Lower**
The life span of the product		
The total indirect labour costs		
Inventory costs		
Infrastructure costs		

44 Which of the following is unlikely to be used when costing digital products?

A Marginal costing

B Absorption costing

C Activity based costing

D Target costing

45 Which of the following is not a typical feature of digital costing?

A Prices are obtained electronically from markets

B Systems are integrated with customer systems

C Intelligence capabilities are built in

D The product cost may constantly change

46 Consider whether the following statements about digital costing are true or false:

	True	**False**
There is a focus on a smaller number of suppliers		
Fewer overhead drivers are used		
Large volumes of data are processed		
The digital cost can be created very quickly		

VARIANCE ANALYSIS

47 A manufacturer expects to use 4 kg of material (at a cost of $5 per kg) on each of its produced units.

Budgeted production was for 5,000 units of a single product. In January, the manufacturer actually spent $82,764 making 4,400 units of its product and used 16,720 kg of material.

To the nearest $, the favourable materials price variance for April is $_______

48 Which of the following best describes a basic standard?

A A standard set at an ideal level, which makes no allowance for normal losses, waste and machine downtime

B A standard which assumes an efficient level of operation, but which includes allowances for factors such as normal loss, waste and machine downtime

C A standard which is kept unchanged over a period of time

D A standard which is based on current price levels

The following data relate to Questions 49 and 50.

X40 is one of many items produced by the manufacturing division. Its standard cost is based on estimated production of 10,000 units per month. The standard cost schedule for one unit of X40 shows that 2 hours of direct labour are required at $15 per labour hour. The variable overhead rate is $6 per direct labour hour. During April, 11,000 units were produced; 24,000 direct labour hours were worked and charged; $336,000 was spent on direct labour; and $180,000 was spent on variable overheads.

---

49 The direct labour rate variance for April is:

A $20,000 Favourable

B $22,000 Favourable

C $24,000 Adverse

D $24,000 Favourable

50 The variable overhead efficiency variance for April is:

A $12,000 Adverse

B $12,000 Favourable

C $15,000 Adverse

D $15,000 Favourable

The following data relate to Questions 51 and 52.

X Ltd operates a standard costing system and absorbs fixed overheads on the basis of machine hours. Details of budgeted and actual figures are as follows:

	Budget	**Actual**
Fixed overheads	\$2,500,000	\$2,010,000
Output	500,000 units	440,000 units
Machine hours	1,000,000 hours	900,000 hours

51 The fixed overhead expenditure variance is

A \$190,000 favourable

B \$250,000 adverse

C \$300,000 adverse

D \$490,000 favourable

52 The fixed overhead volume variance is

A \$190,000 favourable

B \$250,000 adverse

C \$300,000 adverse

D \$490,000 favourable

53 Y has set the current budget for operating costs for its delivery vehicles, using the formula described below. Analysis has shown that the relationship between miles driven and total monthly vehicle operating costs is described in the following formula:

$$y = \$800 + \$0.0002x^2$$

where: y is the total monthly operating cost of the vehicles, and

x is the number of miles driven each month

The budget for vehicle operating costs needs to be adjusted for expected inflation in vehicle operating costs of 3%, which is not included in the relationship shown above.

The delivery mileage for September was 4,100 miles, and the total actual vehicle operating costs for September were \$5,000.

The total vehicle operating cost variance for September was closest to:

A \$713 Adverse

B \$737 Adverse

C \$777 Adverse

D \$838 Adverse

54 L uses a standard costing system. The standard cost card for one of its products shows that the product should use 6 kgs of material P per finished unit, and that the standard price per kg is $6.75. L values its inventory of materials at standard prices.

During November 20X1, when the budgeted production level was 2,000 units, 2,192 units were made. The actual quantity of material P used was 13,050 kgs and material P inventories were reduced by 500 kgs. The cost of the material P which was purchased was $72,900.

The material price and usage variances for November 20X1 were:

	Price	Usage
A	15,185.50 (F)	450.00 (F)
B	11,812.50 (F)	688.50 (F)
C	15,187.50 (F)	450.00 (A)
D	11,812.50 (F)	688.50 (A)

55 A manufacturer spent $244,000 on 9,760 hours of labour producing 6,000 units. However, only 9,480 hours were actually worked by labour. Labour should have taken 1.6 hours per unit at a standard rate of $24 per hour.

What is the value of the adverse labour idle time variance?

A $2,880

B $3,000

C $6,720

D $7,000

56 R Ltd uses a standard costing system and has the following labour cost standard in relation to one of its products:

10 hours skilled labour at $9.50 per hour = $95.00

During March 20X9, 6,200 of these products were made which was 250 units less than budgeted. The labour cost incurred was $596,412 and the number of direct labour hours worked was 62,890. The direct labour variances for the month were:

	Rate	Efficiency
A	$1,043 (F)	$8,900 (A)
B	$7,412 (F)	$8,455 (A)
C	$1,043 (F)	$8,455 (A)
D	$7,412 (F)	$8,900 (A)

57 P Ltd has the following budget and actual data:

Budget fixed overhead cost	$170,000
Budget production (units)	42,500
Actual fixed overhead cost	$182,000
Actual production (units)	40,000

The adverse fixed overhead volume variance is $_______

58 S Ltd has the following budget and actual data:

Budget fixed overhead cost	$1,248,480
Budget production (units)	20,400
Budgeted labour hours	104,040
Actual fixed overhead cost	$1,366,620
Actual production (units)	20,000
Actual labour hours	100,000

The favourable fixed overhead efficiency variance is $_______

The following data relate to Questions 59 and 60.

A hospital uses a standard costing system to monitor the performance of it surgeons. The following information is available for June:

The standard time to perform an eye operation is 2 hours. In June, the budget for eye operations showed that 320 operations would be performed and the (fixed) overheads attributable to eye operations would be $108,000.

The actual results showed that only 300 operations were performed in a total of 660 hours, and that the actual (fixed) overheads were $110,000.

59 **The fixed overhead capacity variance for June was:**

A $3,375 Adverse

B $3,375 Favourable

C $10,125 Favourable

D $10,125 Adverse

60 **The fixed overhead efficiency variance for June was:**

A $3,375 Adverse

B $3,375 Favourable

C $10,125 Favourable

D $10,125 Adverse

61 T Ltd budgets to produce 10,000 units of product D12, each requiring 45 minutes of labour. Labour is charged at $20 per hour, and variable overheads at $15 per labour hour. During September, 11,000 units were produced. 8,000 hours of labour were paid at a total cost of $168,000. Variable overheads in September amounted to $132,000.

What is the variable overhead expenditure variance for September?

A $3,750 Favourable

B $6,125 Favourable

C $12,000 Adverse

D $12,000 Favourable

62 T Ltd budgets to produce 10,000 units of product D12, each requiring 45 minutes of labour. Labour is charged at $20 per hour, and variable overheads at $15 per labour hour. During September, 11,000 units were produced. 8,000 hours of labour were paid at a total cost of $168,000. Variable overheads in September amounted to $132,000.

What is the labour efficiency variance for September?

A $5,000 Adverse

B $5,000 Favourable

C $5,250 Favourable

D $10,000 Adverse

63 Z Ltd sells computers that it purchases through a regional distributor. An extract from its budget for the 4-week period ended 28 March 20X8 shows that it planned to sell 600 computers at a unit price of $500, which would give a contribution to sales ratio of 25%.

Actual sales were 642 computers at an average selling price of $465. The actual contribution to sales ratio averaged 20%.

What was the sales price variance (to the nearest $1)?

A $22,470 (F)

B $1,470 (A)

C $1,470 (F)

D $22,470 (A)

64 Z Ltd sells computers that it purchases through a regional distributor. An extract from its budget for the 4-week period ended 28 March 20X8 shows that it planned to sell 600 computers at a unit price of $500, which would give a contribution to sales ratio of 25%.

Actual sales were 642 computers at an average selling price of $465. The actual contribution to sales ratio averaged 20%.

What was the sales volume contribution variance (to the nearest $1)?

A $5,050 (F)

B $5,150 (F)

C $5,250 (F)

D $5,350 (F)

65 **The fixed overhead volume variance is defined as:**

A the difference between the budgeted value of the fixed overheads and the standard fixed overheads absorbed by actual production

B the difference between the standard fixed overhead cost specified for the production achieved, and the actual fixed overhead cost incurred

C the difference between budgeted and actual fixed overhead expenditure

D the difference between the standard fixed overhead cost specified in the original budget and the same volume of fixed overheads, but at the actual prices incurred

66 **Which of the following events would help to explain an adverse material usage variance (place a tick for all those that apply)?**

		Correct?
(i)	The standard allowance for material wastage was set too high.	
(ii)	Material purchased was of a lower quality than standard.	
(iii)	Lower grade and less experienced employees were used than standard.	
(iv)	More material was purchased than budgeted for the period because output was higher than budgeted.	

67 A retailer uses an activity based budgeting system.

During the month of December, it budgeted for $30,000 of inspection costs at a cost of $200 per inspection. Budgeted volume was 1,000 units. Actual results for December should inspection costs of $34,000 from 160 inspections. Actual volume was 1,200 units.

Using an activity based system, the favourable inspection efficiency variance for December is $_______

68 **Which of the following is the most likely to result in an adverse variable overhead efficiency variance?**

A Higher bonus payments to employees than standard

B Less experienced employees were used than standard

C The use of more expensive, higher quality materials than standard

D Machine power costs per hour were higher than standard

69 PQR Ltd operates a standard absorption costing system. Details of budgeted and actual figures are as follows:

	Budget	**Actual**
Sales volume (units)	100,000	110,000
Selling price per unit	$10	$9.50
Variable cost per unit	$5	$5.25
Total cost per unit	$8	$8.30

The favourable sales volume profit variance for the period was $_______

70 During a period, the staff of A worked 200 hours more than had been planned in the original budget, and 100 hours more than the standard time to produce the actual output. **This would have caused which of the following variances?**

A Favourable labour efficiency variance

B Adverse fixed overhead volume variance

C Favourable fixed overhead efficiency variance

D Favourable fixed overhead capacity variance

71 Q plc uses standard costing. The details for April were as follows:

Budgeted output	15,000	units
Budgeted labour hours	60,000	hours
Budgeted labour cost	$540,000	
Actual output	14,650	units
Actual labour hours paid	61,500	hours
Productive labour hours	56,000	hours
Actual labour cost	$522,750	

The idle time variance for April was $_______

72 **Match the variance with its most likely cause (draw a line connecting the variance to the correct cause)**

Variance
Material price variance
Material usage variance
Labour rate variance
Labour efficiency variance

Cause
Increased wastage due to a machine malfunction
Unexpected pay award
Increase in costs charged by a supplier
Improved operating procedures for staff.

73 **Which two of the following variances are most likely to be directly caused by purchasing better quality materials?**

	Caused by purchasing better quality?
Favourable fixed overhead expenditure variance	
Favourable material usage variance	
Adverse labour rate variance	
Favourable labour efficiency variance	
Favourable labour rate variance	

74 **Which ONE of the following managers is most likely to be responsible for an adverse materials price variance?**

A Production manager

B Purchasing manager

C Human resources manager

D Finance manager

75 **Which ONE of the following managers is most likely to be responsible for an adverse labour efficiency variance?**

A Production manager

B Purchasing manager

C Human resources manager

D Finance manager

76 Which of the following variances would be affected if the company switched from an absorption costing system to a marginal costing system?

	Affected?
Sales price variance	
Sales quantity profit variance	
Fixed overhead expenditure variance	
Fixed overhead capacity variance	

77 AH Ltd uses activity based costing to allocate its overheads. The standard cost expected for the setups cost pool were:

Budgeted units	22,000
Budgeted setups	220
Budgeted cost	$6,820

The Actual costs incurred were

Actual units	21,000
Actual setups	200
Actual cost	$6,300

The expenditure variance for the setups was $______

78 A company produces two products with the following standard information:

	Product X	**Product Y**
Production and sales	10,000 units	18,000 units
Direct labour ($7 per hour)	$14.00	$10.50
Variable overhead	$3.00	$2.25

The company actually spent $87,140 on variable overheads, whilst labour worked for 46,000 hours. 12,000 units of X and 16,000 units of Y were produced.

The favourable variable overhead efficiency variance is $_______

79 A Ltd uses activity based costing to allocate its overheads. The following information is provided for the supervisor cost:

	Budget	**Actual**
Total employees	5,000	5,500
Number of supervisors	75	77
Supervisor cost	$7,500	$8,085

What was the total variance for the supervisor cost?

A $585 Adverse

B $165 Favourable

C $5550 Favourable

D $385 Adverse

80 An audit firm budgeted to provide 60 audits in the next month at a fee of $6,000 each. It actually made total sales of $365,400 from 58 audits.

To the nearest $, the favourable sales price variance is $_______

81 A manufacturer has the following standard information for its audit services:

	$
Standard selling price	50
Standard contribution	20
Standard profit	15
Marginal cost	30

During the year it produced and sold 60,000 units. Budgeted production and sales was 65,000 units. The firm uses a marginal costing system for determining variances.

What will be the value of the adverse sales volume variance for the year?

A $75,000

B $100,000

C $150,000

D $250,000

82 A poster campaign was expected to create 25,000 posters using 6 metres of material per poster which costs $10 per metre.

The actual campaign had 20,000 posters using 122,000 metres of material at a total cost of $1,232,200.

The total adverse materials variance for the campaign was $_______

83 A firm of architects provides standard building evaluations which require 4 hours of skilled labour paid at $60 per hour. During October, 500 evaluations were provided at a total labour cost of $120,900. 1,950 labour hours were used.

The adverse labour rate variance for October is $_______

84 A manufacturer has the following standard cost per unit for labour:

	$
Direct labour(12 minutes)	10

In February the manufacturer spent $2.51m on 50,000 hours of labour. Actual production was 240,000 units.

What is the total labour variance for February?

A $10,000 Favourable

B $10,000 Adverse

C $110,000 Favourable

D $110,000 Adverse

85 An organisation reported actual profit for the month of June of $120,000. The following variances were calculated for the same month:

	$
Materials price variance	2,500 F
Labour efficiency variance	4,000 A
Sales volume variance	7,000 F
Fixed overhead expenditure variance	1,700 A

What was the budgeted profit for June?

A $104,800

B $116,200

C $121,200

D $123,800

FURTHER VARIANCE ANALYSIS

86 SS Ltd operates a standard marginal costing system. An extract from the standard cost card for the labour costs of one of its products is as follows:

Labour cost

5 hours × $12 $60

Actual results for the period were as follows:

Production	11,500 units
Labour rate variance	$45,000 adverse
Labour efficiency variance	$30,000 adverse

The actual rate paid per direct labour hour for the period was $_______

87 During a period, Jones had the following budgeted and actual sales:

	Product A	Product B
Sales budget (units)	800	800
Actual sales (units)	750	700
Standard profit per unit	$5.00	$3.00

The total favourable sales mix profit variance for the period is $_______

88 During a period, A Ltd had the following budgeted and actual sales:

	Product A	Product B	Product C
Sales budget (units)	3,000	8,000	9,000
Actual sales (units)	4,000	7,500	11,500
Standard price per unit	$10.00	$8.00	$5.00
Actual price per unit	$9.50	$8.75	$4.00
Budgeted cost per unit	$8.00	$6.50	$3.20
Actual cost per unit	$8.00	$6.50	$3.20

The total favourable sales quantity profit variance for the period is $_______

89 PQ produces two products, Product B and Product C. The following budget and actual data relate to August:

	Product B	**Product C**
Budget data:		
Production and sales	2,200 units	1,800 units
Standard contribution per unit	$58.00	$59.75
Standard profit per unit	$50.00	$53.75
Actual data:		
Production and sales	3,000 units	1,500 units

The favourable sales mix profit variance for Product B is $_____ (use the individual units method)

90 FF produces two products, Product R and Product S. The following budget and actual data was prepared for the period:

	Product R	**Product S**
Budget data:		
Production and sales	4,000 units	6,000 units
Standard contribution per unit	$6	$8
Standard profit per unit	$4	$3
Actual data:		
Production and sales	6,000 units	6,000 units

The sales quantity profit variance is:

A $0

B $2,720

C $4,080

D $6,800

91 PP Ltd operates a standard absorption costing system. The following information has been extracted from the standard cost card for one of its products:

Budgeted production	1,500 units
Direct material cost: 7 kg × $4.10	$28.70 per unit
Actual results for the period were as follows:	
Production	1,600 units
Direct material (purchased and used): 12,000 kg	$52,200

It has subsequently been noted that, owing to a change in economic conditions, the best price that the material could have been purchased for was $4.50 per kg during the period.

The adverse material price planning variance was $______

92 The materials price variance for the month of January was $2,000 favourable and the usage variance was $450 favourable. The standard material usage per unit is 6 kg, and the standard material price is $3.00 per kg. 600 units were produced in the period and there was no change in inventory levels during the period.

Material purchases in the period were:

A 2,000 kg

B 2,933 kg

C 3,450 kg

D 3,600 kg

93 The following data relate to Product Z and its raw material content for September:

Budget

Output	11,000 units of Z
Standard materials content	3 kg per unit at $4.00 per kg

Actual

Output	10,000 units of Z
Materials purchased and used	32,000 kg at $4.80 per kg

It has now been agreed that the standard price for the raw material purchased in September should have been $5 per kg.

What was the materials operational price variance for September?

A $6,000 Adverse

B $6,400 Favourable

C $30,000 Adverse

D $32,000 Adverse

94 The following data relate to Product Z and its raw material content for September:

Budget

Output	11,000 units of Z
Standard materials content	3 kg per unit at $4.00 per kg

Actual

Output	10,000 units of Z
Materials purchased and used	32,000 kg at $4.80 per kg

It has now been agreed that the standard price for the raw material purchased in September should have been $5 per kg.

Using actual units produced, what was the materials planning price variance for September?

A $6,000 Adverse

B $30,000 Adverse

C $32,000 Adverse

D $33,000 Adverse

95 During a period, J Ltd had the following budgeted and actual sales:

	Product A	**Product B**
Sales budget (units)	800	800
Actual sales (units)	750	700
Standard profit per unit	$5.00	$3.00

The total adverse sales quantity profit variance for the period is $______

96 The following data relate to Product Z and its raw material content for September:

Budget

Output	11,000 units of Z
Standard materials content	3 kg per unit at $4.00 per kg

Actual

Output	10,000 units of Z
Materials purchased and used	32,000 kg at $4.80 per kg

It has now been agreed that the standard price for the raw material purchased in September should have been $5 per kg.

What was the materials operational usage variance for September?

A $8,000 Adverse

B $9,600 Adverse

C $9,600 Favourable

D $10,000 Adverse

97 PP Ltd operates a standard absorption costing system. The following information has been extracted from the standard cost card for one of its products:

Budgeted production	1,500 units
Direct material cost: 7 kg × $4.10	$28.70 per unit

Actual results for the period were as follows:

Production	1,600 units
Direct material (purchased and used): 12,000 kg	$52,200

It has subsequently been noted that, owing to a change in economic conditions, the best price that the material could have been purchased for was $4.50 per kg during the period.

The adverse operational material usage variance was $______

98 A museum has a new temporary exhibition for which it has budgeted for the following sales:

	Full Price Tickets	Concessions
Volume	9,000	3,000
Contribution per unit	$9	$4

Actual sales were as follows:

	Full Price Tickets	Concessions
Volume	12,000	8,000
Contribution per unit	$9	$5

To the nearest $, using the individual units method, the favourable sales mix variance for concessions for the exhibition is $_______

99 Operation B, in a factory, has a standard time of 15 minutes. The standard rate of pay for operatives is $10 per hour. The budget for a period was based on carrying out the operation 350 times. It was subsequently realised that the standard time for Operation B included in the budget did not incorporate expected time savings from the use of new machinery from the start of the period. The standard time should have been reduced to 12 minutes.

Operation B was actually carried out 370 times in the period in a total of 80 hours. The operatives were paid $850.

The operational labour efficiency variance was:

A $60 adverse

B $75 favourable

C $100 adverse

D $125 adverse

100 A car manufacturer sells two versions of the same vehicle.

	Diesel-powered	Electric-powered
Standard selling price per car	$30,000	$40,000
Standard variable cost per car	$25,000	$36,000

The actual sales of the diesel-powered car were the same as the budget but the actual sales of the electric-powered car were lower than budgeted.

What sales variances would the car manufacturer have?

A An adverse sales mix contribution variance and an adverse sales quantity contribution variance

B An adverse sales mix contribution variance and a favourable sales quantity contribution variance

C A favourable sales mix contribution variance and an adverse sales quantity contribution variance

D A favourable sales mix contribution variance and a favourable sales quantity contribution variance

101 A company operates a standard absorption costing system. The following fixed production overhead data are available for the latest period:

Budgeted output	300,000 units
Budgeted fixed production overhead	$1,500,000
Actual fixed production overhead	$1,950,000
Fixed production overhead total variance	$150,000 adverse

The actual level of production for the period was _______ units (round to the nearest 1,000 units)

102 A firm budgeted for material costs of $54,000 in May. Material was expected to cost $6 per kg each unit was expected to use 2 kg of material.

The actual cost of material in May was $56,000 and there was an adverse material price variance of $4,220.

The actual quantity of materials purchased in May was _______ kg

103 An accountancy firm uses part-qualified accountants in the preparation of sole trader accounts. The firm budgeted to complete 150 sets of sole trader accounts in the period at a standard time of 10 hours for each set. Due to a shortage of available part-qualified accountants in the market-place during the period, the firm was forced to use senior accountants for the completion of the sole trader accounts and it is estimated that this has reduced the time taken to complete each set of by 25%. The senior accountants completed 200 sets of sole trader accounts in the period, taking a total of 1,400 hours.

Which TWO of the following statements are correct?

A The planning variance is adverse

B The operational labour efficiency variance is favourable

C The operational labour rate variance is favourable

D The operational labour efficiency variance is the difference between 1,400 hours and 2,000 hours, charged at the standard hourly labour rate

E The operational labour efficiency variance is the difference between the actual time taken to complete the accounts and the revised standard time for actual output, charged at the standard hourly labour rate

BUDGETING AND BUDGETARY CONTROL

PREPARING BUDGETS

104 Which of the following can be identified as purposes of budgeting (tick all that apply)?

	Purpose of budgeting?
Communication	
Authorisation	
Sales maximisation	
Co-ordination	

105 Which of the following statements regarding budgeting is NOT true?

A Functional budgets should be prepared before the master budget

B The cash budget is not part of the master budget

C Functional budgeting should start with the budget for the principal budget factor

D The production budget is needed before the material usage budget can be prepared

106 A manufacturer sells its sole product at $200 per unit. It has the following budgeted sales for the next three quarters:

Quarter	1	2	3
Sales ($000)	500	600	800

It has a policy of maintaining inventory at 10% of the following quarter's sales volume.

What is the number of units to be produced in quarter 2?

A 620 units

B 2,900 units

C 3,000 units

D 3,100 units

107 PP Ltd is preparing the production and material purchases budgets for one of their products, the S, for the forthcoming year.

The following information is available:

Sales demand (units)	30,000
Material usage per unit	7 kgs
Estimated opening inventory	3,500 units
Required closing inventory	35% higher than opening inventory

How many units of the S will need to be produced?

A 28,775

B 30,000

C 31,225

D 38,225

108 Which of the following is not a typical problem that organisations may face when dealing with big data?

A The increasing use of electronic devices within society at large

B A lack of skills in the labour pool relating to the handling of big data

C Legal and privacy issues if data is held about individuals

D Measurement of metrics that have no use to the organisation

109 EFG uses an Activity Based Budgeting system. It manufactures three products, budgeted details of which are set out below:

	Product E	**Product F**	**Product G**
Budgeted annual production (units)	75,000	120,000	60,000
Batch size (units)	200	60	30
Machine set-ups per batch	5	3	9

Three cost pools have been identified. Budgeted machine set-up costs for the year are $180,000.

The budgeted machine set-up cost per unit of product F is $_______

110 An incremental budgeting system is:

A a system which budgets only for the extra costs associated with a particular plan

B a system which budgets for the variable manufacturing costs only

C a system which prepares budgets only after the manager responsible has justified the continuation of the relevant activity

D a system which prepares budgets by adjusting the previous year's values by expected changes in volumes of activity and price/inflation effects

111 A company has the following expected sales for the next three months of the year:

April	12,000 units
May	15,000 units
June	18,000 units

The opening inventory of the product in April is expected to be 3,600 units.

At the end of each month closing inventory is expected to equal 30% of the following month's sales.

The expected level of production in May is ______ units

112 Which of the following is a common feature of a beyond budgeting approach?

A A greater use of rolling budgets

B A greater use of top-down budgets

C A greater emphasis on financial targets

D A greater focus on standardisation

113 Which of the following definitions best describes 'Zero-Based Budgeting'?

A A method of budgeting where an attempt is made to make the expenditure under each cost heading as close to zero as possible.

B A method of budgeting whereby all activities are re-evaluated each time a budget is formulated.

C A method of budgeting that recognises the difference between the behaviour of fixed and variable costs with respect to changes in output and the budget is designed to change appropriately with such fluctuations.

D A method of budgeting where the sum of revenues and expenditures in each budget centre must equal zero.

114 N Ltd is preparing its sales budget. Estimated sales are 120,000 units if the summer is rainy, and 80,000 units if the summer is dry. The probability of a dry summer is 0.4.

What is the expected value for sales volume?

A 96,000 units

B 100,000 units

C 104,000 units

D 120,000 units

115 Identify which of the following statements about big data are true or false?

	True	**False**
Big data management involves using sophisticated systems to gather, store and analyse large volumes of data		
Data can be a variety of structured and unstructured formats.		
Big data does not include traditional data from internal sources such as sales history, preferences, order frequency and pricing information.		
Big data does include information from external sources such as websites, trade publications and social networks.		

116 Which of the following items would not be included in cash budget:

A cost of acquiring fixtures and fittings

B cost of maintaining fixtures and fittings

C proceeds from the sale of fixtures and fittings

D profit on disposal of fixtures and fittings

117 K has determined a cost driver rate for quality testing as $850 per test.

During the year there were actually on average 50 tests per month, giving an adverse variance on the total cost for quality testing of $102,000 for the year.

The budgeted cost per month for quality testing is $_______

118 A master budget comprises the:

A budgeted income statement and budgeted cash flow only

B budgeted income statement and budgeted balance sheet only

C budgeted income statement and budgeted capital expenditure only

D budgeted income statement, budgeted balance sheet and budgeted cash flow only

119 D plc operates a retail business. Purchases are sold at cost plus 25%. The management team is preparing the cash budget and has gathered the following data:

1 The budgeted sales are as follows:

Month	$000
July	100
August	90
September	125

2 It is management policy to hold inventory at the end of each month which is sufficient to meet sales demand in the next half month. Sales are budgeted to occur evenly during each month.

3 Creditors are paid one month after the purchase has been made.

The entry for 'purchases' that will be shown in the cash budget for August is $_____

120 A company has the following budgeted sales figures:

Month 1	$105,000
Month 2	$120,000
Month 3	$108,000

80% of sales are on credit and the remainder are paid in cash. Credit customers paying within one month are given a discount of 1.5%. Credit customers normally pay within the following time frame:

Within 1 month	40% of credit sales
Within 2 months	98% of credit sales

There is an expectation that 2% of credit sales will become irrecoverable (bad) debts.

Outstanding receivables at the beginning of month 1 includes $6,000 expected to be received in month 3.

The total receipts expected in month 3 are $_______

121 CJD Ltd manufactures plastic components for the car industry and uses activity-based budgeting. The actual number of customer deliveries for each of the three products for the last period were as follows:

	W	**X**	**Y**
Actual number of customer deliveries	1,200	1,800	2,000

The actual delivery costs were $1,400,000.

CJD is preparing next period's budget and has forecast the following:

	W	**X**	**Y**
Forecast number of customer deliveries	1,400	1,900	2,200

The average cost per delivery is expected to increase by 10% due to increases in fuel cost.

The total budgeted delivery cost for the next period is $______

122 QR Ltd manufacturers three products, Product A, Product B and Product C. The following information is available from the company's draft activity-based budget for next year:

	A	**B**	**C**	**Total**
Total number of product inspections	800	1,500	2,200	4,500
Cost per inspection				
$45,000 / 4,500 inspections = $10				
Budgeted inspection costs	$8,000	$15,000	$22,000	$45,000

Inspection costs are a semi-variable cost, partly-driven by the number of inspections.

The product manager responsible for Product C is unhappy about amount of inspection costs which have been allocated to Product C and is planning to significantly reduce the number of inspections of Product C before the final version of the activity-based budget is agreed.

Which of the following would not happen as a result of the decision to inspect less items of Product C?

A a decrease in the amount of inspection costs allocated to Products A and B

B a decrease in the amount of inspections costs allocated to Product C

C a decrease in total inspection costs

D a decrease in the number of customer returns for Product C

123 JB has budgeted production for the next budget year of 36,000 units. Each unit of production requires 4 labour hours and the budgeted labour rate is $12 per hour excluding overtime. Idle time is expected to be 10% of total hours available i.e. including idle time. Due to labour shortages it is expected that 20% of the hours paid, including idle time, will be paid at an overtime rate of time and a half.

The labour cost budget for the year is $______

124 Each finished units of Product Y takes 2 hours of direct labour at a rate of $10 per hour. Budgeted data for the next period are as follows:

Production of Product Y	1,800 units
Idle time	10% of total labour time

The direct labour cost budget for the period is $_______

125 AB is preparing its cash budget for next year. The accounts receivable at the beginning of next year are expected to be $460,000. The budgeted sales are $5,400,000 and will occur evenly throughout the year. 80% of the budgeted sales will be on credit and the remainder will be cash sales. Credit customers pay in the month following sale.

The budgeted cash receipts from customers next year are:

A $5,040,000

B $5,410,000

C $5,500,000

D $5,890,000

126 A wedding company provides two wedding packages, the Silver and the Gold. Budgeted information for the forthcoming year is as follows:

	Silver	**Gold**
Sales volume	400	200
	$	$
Sales revenue	400,000	400,000
Variable costs	160,000	200,000
Contribution	240,000	200,000

The director wishes to change the sales mix so that, whilst total sales revenue remains the same, the sales mix (by revenue) is 25% Silver and 75% Gold.

The revised budgeted contribution from Gold packages is $_______

127 A nursery has produced the following budget for next year

	$
Fee income	150,000
Staff costs	(65,625)
Other direct costs	(28,125)
Overhead costs	(42,188)
	———
Profit	14,062

The nursery manager wants to stress test the budget for a potential change in staff costs, as it is rumoured that a new nursery is opening nearby which is offering a higher hourly rate to recruit staff. The manager is considering increasing its staff wages by 4% at the upcoming appraisals in a bid to prevent staff from leaving.

If the manager increased wages by 4%, the revised gross profit next year would fall by _______ % (answer to 2 d.p.)

128 Big data can be difficult to manage for a variety of reasons. These can be summarised using the 4 Vs.

Which of the following correctly describes volume?

A The speed at which data is generated

B The quantity of the data that is generated

C The range of data that is generated

D The accuracy of the data that is generated

129 **Match the following costs to the correct budget (draw a line connecting the cost to the correct budget)**

Cost
Commission paid to an agent for selling the product
Electricity used in the factory
Depreciation of factory building
Packaging material to protect the product

Budget
Distribution overhead budget
Variable production overhead budget
Selling overhead budget
Fixed production overhead budget

130 D plc operates a retail business. Purchases are sold at cost plus 25%. The management team is preparing the cash budget and has gathered the following data:

1 The budgeted sales are as follows:

Month	$000
August	90
September	125
October	140

2 It is management policy to hold inventory at the end of each month which is sufficient to meet sales demand in the next half month. Sales are budgeted to occur evenly during each month.

3 Creditors are paid one month after the purchase has been made.

The entry for 'purchases' that will be shown in the cash budget for September is $_____

131 AB is preparing its cash budget for next year. The estimated accounts payable balance at the beginning of next year is $540,000. The budgeted purchases for next year are $6,800,000, occurring evenly throughout the year. It is estimated that 75% of purchases will be on credit and the remainder will be for cash. The company pays for credit purchases in the month following purchase.

The budgeted cash payments to suppliers next year are:

A $6,375,000

B $6,773,333

C $6,915,000

D $5,215,000

132 Which of the following would be included in the fixed production overhead budget?

A The annual salary of a supervisor that monitors the performance of factory workers

B The annual rent charged on the head office building

C The annual variable electricity usage charge of the factory machinery used to make the product

D The annual cost of materials used to make the product

133 The following costs have been estimated for the following period.

Direct material	$20,000
Electricity	$8,750
Indirect labour	$37,500
Rent	$6,000
Royalty fee	$2,150

What would be the total overhead budget for the period?

A $74,000

B $72,250

C $52,250

D $14,750

134 During a period, A Ltd expected to produce 5,000 units using 16,000 labour hours and 9,000 machine hours.

If the budgeted overhead absorption rate was $12.50 per labour hour, the budgeted fixed overheads in the period were $_______

135 The following budgeted information comes from the accounting records of ABC

	Product A	**Product B**
Production units	1,000	2,000
Labour hours per unit	0.5 hours	2 hours
Machine hours per unit	0.25 hours	1.5 hours
Variable overhead rate (per machine hour)	$1.50 per hour	
Fixed overhead rate (per labour hour)	$1.95 per hour	

What would be the total overhead budget for the period?

A $11,625

B $13,088

C $13,650

D $15,113

136 **Which TWO of the following are NOT criticisms of incremental budgeting?**

	Not a criticism?
It may make managers, staff and unions feel threatened	
It encourages slack	
It is time consuming as it involves starting from scratch	
It encourages wasteful spending	
It includes past inefficiencies as costs are not scrutinised	

137 Which two of the following are NOT characteristics of rolling budgets?

	Characteristic of rolling budgets?
Budgets are more likely to be realistic as there is a shorter period between preparation and actual events occurring	
Updates to budgets are only made when they are foreseeable	
They reduce uncertainty in budgeting	
They force management to look ahead more frequently	
Each item of expenditure must be fully justified before inclusion in the budget	

138 Which ONE of the following best describes incremental budgeting?

A Increments of income and expenditure are compared with forecasted results

B A method of budgeting where all activities are re-evaluated each time a budget is formulated

C A budget updated in regular increments by adding a further accounting period when the earliest period has expired

D The budget for each period is based on prior period results, modified for changes in activity levels

139 The following is a description of which method of budgeting?

'A budget continuously updated by adding a further accounting period when the earliest accounting period has expired.'

A Zero based budgeting

B Activity based budgeting

C Incremental budgeting

D Rolling budgets

140 LF has the following expected production for the next three months:

Month	**1**	**2**	**3**
	unit	units	units
Production	1,850	1,800	2,020

The variable production overhead cost per unit is $1.20. 60% of these will be paid in the month in which production occurs and the remainder will be paid one month later.

What will be the variable overhead payment in month 2?

A $2,160

B $2,424

C $1,296

D $2,184

141 RF has prepared the following sales forecast for its first three months of trading:

Month	Number of components
1	1,500
2	1,750
3	2,000

The selling price has been set at $10 per component in the first three months.

Sales receipts

Time of payment	% of customers
Month of sale	20*
One month later	45
Two months later	25
Three months later	5

The balance represents anticipated bad debts.

*A 2% discount is given to customers for payment received in the month of sale.

The sales receipts for month 2 are budgeted to be $______

142 A manufacturer has produced the following budget for the upcoming year

	$000
Revenue	720
Cost of sales	324
Other operating costs	120
Net profit	276

The directors are concerned about the potential loss of a major customer and wish to stress test the budget for such a loss. The customer accounts for 30% of the company's total sales revenue and provides a gross mark-up of 20% on cost.

What would be the revised budgeted profit if the customer's sales were lost?

A $157,200

B $232,800

C $240,000

D $360,000

FORECASTING

143 The following details relate to the total cost of product X in two accounting periods:

Number of units	500	800
	$	$
Direct materials	1,000	1,600
Direct labour	750	1,200
Production overhead	1,250	1,400
Other overhead	500	500
	3,500	4,700

The fixed cost per period and variable cost per unit are:

	Fixed costs	**Variable cost/unit**
	$	$
A	1,000	1.125
B	1,000	4.00
C	1,500	3.50
D	1,500	4.00

144 Z plc has found that it can estimate future sales using time series analysis and regression techniques. The following trend equation has been derived:

y = 25,000 + 6,500x

where

y is the total sales units per quarter

x is the time period reference number

Z has also derived the following set of seasonal variation index values for each quarter using a multiplicative (proportional) model:

Quarter 1	70%
Quarter 2	90%
Quarter 3	150%
Quarter 4	90%

Assuming that the first quarter of year 1 is time period reference number 1. What would be the forecast sales units for the third quarter of year 7?

A 174,500 units

B 200,500 units

C 261,750 units

D 300,750 units

145 H plc is mobile phone repair shop. The director is interested in the relationship between the amount that is spent on advertising and the sales revenue that is achieved. He/she/they have established that the regression equation y = 150 + 7x can be used, where y is the total sales revenue and x is the advertising spend (in $000s).

Which ONE of the following statements is a correct interpretation of the relationship?

A If $7,000 is spent on advertising, then sales revenue would be $150,000

B If no money is spent on advertising, then sales revenue would be $7,000

C If $150,000 is spent on advertising, then $7,000 sales revenue per month will be generated

D If no money is spent on advertising, then sales revenue would be $150,000

146 Production overhead costs at company MZ Ltd are assumed to vary in line with the number of labour hours worked. The following data has been collected:

Year	**Total production overheads** $	**Number of labour hours**	**Cost index**
20X4	205,000	4,200	189
20X5	226,180	4,700	205

If the line of best fit, based on current (20X5) prices is calculated as y = 127,000 + 18.6x, calculate the total expected overhead costs in 20X6 if expected production activity is 4,600 labour hours and the expected cost index is 225.

A $193,666

B $212,560

C $233,298

D $253,048

147 A company is estimating its cost of production wages based on past information using the high-low method to separate total costs into their fixed and variable elements. The total wage costs incurred by the company in the previous two months were as follows:

Month	**Labour hours worked**	**Total costs** $
1	160,000	2,420,000
2	190,000	2,982,000

In Month 2, all employees were given a 5% pay rise.

What is the variable labour cost per hour for Month 3?

A $14.00

B $14.70

C $18.73

D $23.70

148 The overhead costs of RP have been found to be accurately represented by the formula:

$$y = \$10,000 + \$0.25x$$

where y is the monthly cost and x represents the activity level measured as the number of orders.

Monthly activity levels of orders may be estimated using a combined regression analysis and time series model:

$$a = 100,000 + 30b$$

where a represents the de-seasonalised monthly activity level and b represents the month number. In month 240, the seasonal index value is 108.

The overhead cost for RP for month 240 is $_______ (round to the nearest $1,000)

149 Monthly sales of product R follow a linear trend of $y = 9.72 + 5.816x$, where y is the number of units sold and x is the number of the month. Monthly deviations from the trend follow an additive model.

The forecast number of units of product R to be sold in month 23, which has a seasonal factor of +6.5 is, to the nearest whole unit:

A 134

B 137

C 143

D 150

150 H is forecasting its sales for next year using a combination of time series and regression analysis models. An analysis of past sales units has produced the following equation for the quarterly sales trend:

$y = 26x + 8,850$

where the value of x represents the quarterly accounting period and the value of y represents the quarterly sales trend in units. Quarter 1 of next year will have a value for x of 25.

The quarterly seasonal variations have been measured using the multiplicative model and are:

Quarter 1	– 15%
Quarter 2	– 5%
Quarter 3	+ 5%
Quarter 4	+ 15%

Production is planned to occur at a constant rate throughout the year. The company does not hold inventories at the end of any year.

What is the difference between the budgeted sales for quarter 1 and quarter 4 next year?

A 78 units

B 2,850 units

C 2,862 units

D 2,940 units

151 The following budgeted information comes from the accounting records of R Ltd

Production units	1,000	2,000	3,000
	$	$	$
Material cost	15,000	30,000	45,000
Labour cost	10,000	20,000	30,000
Overhead cost	18,000	22,000	26,000
Distribution cost	12,000	12,000	12,000
Total cost	55,000	84,000	113,000

What would be the budgeted cost for 2,750 units?

A $103,583

B $105,750

C $106,750

D $109,250

152 A company has calculated that the coefficient of determination between output and production costs over a number of months is 89%.

Which TWO of the following comments are correct?

	Correct?
89% of the variation in production costs from one month to the next can be explained by corresponding variation in output.	
Costs increase as output increases.	
The linear relationship between output and costs is very strong.	
An increase of 100% in output is associated with an increase of 89% in costs.	
An increase of 89% in output is associated with an increase of 100% in costs.	

153 The following budgeted information comes from the accounting records of J Ltd

Production units	1,000	2,000
Budgeted materials cost	$18,000	$24,000
Cost index	100	125

J Ltd wants to determine the estimated materials cost for the next month when it is expected to produce 2,600 units and the cost index is expected to be 142.

What is the budgeted cost of materials for next month, where production is expected to be 2,600 units? (to the nearest $)

A $19,920

B $27,600

C $28,286

D $39,192

154 Which of the following statements relating to linear regression are correct? Select all that apply.

A It assumes a linear relationship between the variables

B It is useful where we are measuring the relationship between more than two variables

C It assumes that the historical behaviour of the data continues into the future

D It can be used reliably for interpolation and extrapolation

E It can be used reliably where there is no correlation between the data

155 A company has identified the trend in its sales figures through the regression equation y = 1,450 + 55x, where y is the sales revenue and x is the quarter number. For quarter 1 of year 1, x = 1. The average seasonal variation for quarter 2 is 115%.

Calculate the forecast sales revenue for quarter 2 in Year 2.

A $1,668

B $1,780

C $1,794

D $2,047

BUDGETARY CONTROL

156 Which two of the following are limitations of sensitivity analysis in cash budgeting?

	Limitations of sensitivity analysis?
Only one variable changes at a time	
It assesses the risk to the closing cash balance	
It provides an assessment of how responsive the cash flows are to changes in variables	
Probabilities of changes are not accounted for	
It directs attention to critical variables	

157 Which of the following best describes 'budgetary slack'?

A The difference between what has been set as a budgetary objective and what has been achieved for the period

B The demotivating impact of a budgetary target that has been set too high

C The deliberate over-estimation of expenditure and/or under-estimation of revenues in the budgetary planning process

D Accumulated favourable variances reported against a specific item of budgeted expenditure

158 A retailer has prepared the following budget for one country where it operates in 20 locations:

	$000
Revenue	6,800
Cost of sales	4,500
Other operating costs	1,600
Net profit	700

The retailer wants to test what impact would be seen on profit if revenue was to fall by 40%. It expects that it would save $400,000 on rent by closing stores but would have to pay $250,000 in redundancy costs to affected staff. Cost of sales are believed to be 80% variable and 20% fixed.

What would be the fall in profit for the year?

A $430

B $1,170

C $1,130

D $1,870

159 M Ltd had the following budget and actual results during a period:

	Original budget	**Actual**
Sales units	1,000	1,380
	$	$
Sales revenue	100,000	133,860
Direct material	40,000	57,800
Direct labour	20,000	27,000
Variable overhead	15,000	18,600
Fixed overhead	10,000	11,000
Profit	15,000	19,460

Using a flexed budget approach, the total adverse profit variance for the period is $_______

160 **A flexible budget is best defined as**

A A budget for a single level of activity that does not change in a period

B A budget that is based on zero expenditure and is only increased if the expenditure is fully justified

C A budget for the number of units that were actually sold during a period

D A budget that can be restated to any level of output

161 X Co uses rolling budgeting, updating its budgets on a quarterly basis. After carrying out the last quarter's update to the cash budget, it projected a forecast cash deficit of $400,000 at the end of the year. Consequently, the planned purchase of new capital equipment has been postponed.

Which of the following types of control is the sales manager's actions an example of?

A Feedforward control

B Negative feedback control

C Positive feedback control

D Double loop feedback control

162 The following budgeted information comes from the accounting records of S Ltd

	Original budget
Sales units	1,000
	$
Sales revenue	100,000
Direct material	40,000
Direct labour	20,000
Variable overhead	15,000
Fixed overhead	10,000
Profit	15,000

In a period where the actual sales were 1,200 units, what would be the flexed budget?

A $17,000

B $20,000

C $22,000

D $35,000

163 What ONE of the following is the purpose of a flexible budget?

A To compare actual and budgeted results at virtually any level of production

B To reduce the total time in preparing the annual budget

C To allow management some latitude in meeting goals

D To eliminate cyclical fluctuations in production reports by ignoring variable costs

164 Which ONE of the following is an advantage of non-participative budgeting as compared to participative budgeting?

A It increases motivation

B It is less time consuming

C It increases acceptance

D The budgets produced are more attainable

165 Which ONE of the following is not an impact caused by unethical behaviour in the budgeting system?

A Damage to an organisation's share price caused by over-stating actual results

B Damage to an organisation's reputation due to poor treatment of budget holders

C Budget holders encouraging staff to ignore unattainable budget targets

D Budget holders using aggressive policies to achieve targeted results

166 A law firm has forecast its cash balances for the next six months as follows:

Month	**1**	**2**	**3**	**4**	**5**	**6**
	$000	$000	$000	$000	$000	$000
Net cash flow	80	120	(250)	(260)	400	320
Opening cash balance	200	280	400	150	(110)	290
Closing cash balance	280	400	150	(110)	290	610

Employees are paid in the month that they perform work. The firm have taken on a new client where work will be performed in month 3 and the customer is expected to pay its $300,000 invoice in month 4. This work is invoiced at a 50% mark up on labour costs (the only directly attributable cost for the client work).

The firm have an overdraft limit of $250,000 and want to test whether the limit will be breached if the customer fails to pay for the work performed.

If the customer does not pay their invoice by how much will the overdraft be exceeded in month 4?

A $0

B $110,000

C $160,000

D $410,000

167 A retailer has forecast receipts for its first three months of operations as follows:

Month	**Jan**	**Feb**	**March**
Sales (Units × $40)	60,000	70,000	40,000
Paid in month – 20% × 0.95	11,400	13,300	7,600
50% in the following month		30,000	35,000
30% in 3rd month			18,000
Receipts	11,400	43,300	60,600

Customers who pay in the month of sales will receive a 5% settlement discount. As part of the retailer's sensitivity analysis it wants to examine the impact on receipts if only 15% of customers pay in the month of sales (with 55% of customers paying in the month following the sale.

The revised cash receipts in March would be $_______

168 Consider whether following statement regarding feed-forward control budgetary systems are true or false:

	True	False
Feed-forward control systems have an advantage over other types of control in that it establishes how effective planning was.		
Feed-forward control occurs while an activity is in progress.		

169 A manufacturer has prepared a production budget for the next three months (based on the new assumption that closing inventory would be 20% of the next month's sales) as follows:

Production budget (units)	**June**	**July**	**August**
Sales	14,000	9,000	12,000
Add closing inventory	1,800	2,400	3,000
Less opening inventory	3,600	1,800	2,400
Production	12,200	9,600	12,600

The manufacturer wants to perform some sensitivity analysis on the basis that the inventory level is reduced to 10% of the following month's sales.

The new budgeted production in July would be _______ units.

170 Which of the following costs should the manager of the purchasing department have his/her/their performance appraised on?

Select all that apply.

A The price paid for raw materials

B The annual rental cost of the factory

C The advertising campaigns for new product launches

D The wages paid to employees in the purchasing department

171 Which TWO of the following statements in relation to budgetary control are true?

A Unrealistic targets are likely to adversely affect a manager's performance

B Budgetary control ensures goal congruence

C Budgetary control should take place annually

D Budgetary control may result in increased motivation

SHORT-TERM COMMERCIAL DECISION MAKING

RELEVANT COSTS AND DECISION MAKING

172 An organisation is considering the costs to be incurred in respect of a special order opportunity.

The order would require 1,250 kgs of material D. This is a material that is readily available and regularly used by the organisation on its normal products. There are 265 kgs of material D in stock which cost $795 last week. The current market price is $3.24 per kg.

Material D is normally used to make product X. Each unit of X requires 3 kgs of material D, and if material D is costed at $3 per kg, each unit of X yields a contribution of $15.

What is the relevant cost of material D to be included in the costing of the special order?

A $3,990

B $4,050

C $10,000

D $10,300

173 H Ltd has in stock 15,000 kg of M, a raw material which it bought for $3/kg five years ago, for a product line which was discontinued four years ago.

At present, M has no use in its existing state but could be sold as scrap for $1.00 per kg. One of the company's current products (HN) requires 4 kg of a raw material which is available for $5.00 per kg. M can be modified at a cost of $0.75 per kg so that it may be used as a substitute for this material. However, after modification, 5 kg of M is required for every unit of HN to be produced.

H Ltd has now received an invitation to tender for a product which could use M in its present state.

What is the relevant cost per kg of M to be included in the cost estimate for the tender?

A $0.75

B $1.00

C $3.00

D $3.25

174 J Ltd is bidding for a contract which is due to be started within a few days. The contract will use up its stock of Material XY which will otherwise be held for one month. In one month's time, there is a probability of 0.6 that it will be used. If it is not used, then the material will be sold. Estimates are as follows:

	$
Replacement cost of stock in one month's time	15,000
Sales value in one month's time	12,000
Stock holding cost for one month	900

The expected relevant cost of Material XY for use when evaluating the viability of the contract is $_______

175 UU Company has been asked to quote for a special contract which will require material X. The following information is available on material X:

Book value	Scrap value	Replacement cost
$5.00 per kg	$0.50 per kg	$5.50 per kg

The special contract would require 10 kgs of Material X. There are 250 kgs of this material in stock which was purchased in error over two years ago. It has just been noticed that if Material X is modified, at a cost of $2 per kg, it could then be used as a substitute for material Y which is in regular use and currently costs $6 per kg.

The relevant cost of the materials for the special contract is:

A $5

B $40

C $50

D $55

176 A company has been asked to quote for a special contract. The following information is available regarding the labour required for the contract:

The special contract would require 100 hours of labour. However, the labourers, who are each paid $15 per hour, are working at full capacity. There is a shortage of labour in the market and therefore the labour required to undertake this special contract would have to be taken from another contract, Z, which currently utilises 500 hours of labour and generates $5,000 worth of contribution. If the labour was taken from contract Z, then the whole of contract Z would have to be delayed, and such delay would invoke a penalty fee of $1,000.

What is the relevant cost of labour?

A $1,000

B $1,500

C $2,500

D $7,500

177 A company is preparing a quotation for a one-month consultancy project. Currently the company employs a consultant on an annual salary of $36,000.

This consultant is fully employed on current projects and, if he/she/they were to be transferred to this new project, then an existing junior consultant would be used to cover his/her/their current work. The junior consultant would be paid a bonus of $5,000 for undertaking this additional responsibility.

Alternatively, the company could hire an external consultant on a one-month contract at a cost of $4,500.

The relevant cost to be used in preparing the quotation is:

A $4,500

B $5,000

C $40,500

D $41,000

178 In order to utilise some spare capacity, K Ltd is preparing a quotation for a special order which requires 2,000 kgs of material J.

K Ltd has 800 kgs of material J in stock (original cost $7.00 per kg). Material J is used in the company's main product L. Each unit of L uses 5 kgs of material J and, based on an input value of $7.00 per kg of J, each unit of L yields a contribution of $10.00.

The resale value of material J is $5.50 per kg. The present replacement price of material J is $8.00 per kg. Material J is readily available in the market.

The relevant cost of the 2,000 kgs of material J to be included in the quotation is $_______

179 Which of the following statements is NOT an advantage of acting ethically in business decision making?

A The organisation will become more attractive to stakeholders

B Global organisations can have a consistent global approach to decision making

C Business risk can be reduced

D The risk of regulatory breaches is reduced

180 A company is calculating the relevant cost of the material to be used on a particular contract.

The contract requires 4,200 kgs of material H and this can be bought for $6.30 per kg.

The company bought 10,000 kgs of material H some time ago when it paid $4.50 per kg. Currently 3,700 kgs of this remains in inventory. The inventory of material H could be sold for $3.20 per kg.

The company has no other use for material H other than on this contract, but it could modify it at a cost of $3.70 per kg and use it as a substitute for material J. Material J is regularly used by the company and can be bought for $7.50 per kg.

The relevant cost of the material for the contract is:

A $17,210

B $19,800

C $26,460

D $30,900

181 Which of the following accounting entries is ignored when making decisions based on relevant costs and revenues?

A Increases to pension cost provisions

B Reductions in loans

C Increases in non-current assets

D Reductions in working capital

182 P Limited is considering whether to continue making a component or buy it from an outside supplier. It uses 12,000 of the components each year.

The internal manufacturing cost comprises:

	$/unit
Direct materials	3.00
Direct labour	4.00
Variable overhead	1.00
Specific fixed cost	2.50
Other fixed costs	2.00
	12.50

If the direct labour were not used to manufacture the component, it would be used to increase the production of another item for which there is unlimited demand. This other item has a contribution of $10.00 per unit but requires $8.00 of labour per unit.

The maximum price per component at which buying is preferable to internal manufacture is:

A $8.00

B $10.50

C $12.50

D $15.50

183 A company manufactures two joint products and a by-product in a single process, which are all sold as soon as they are output from the process, without further processing. Joint costs are shared on the basis of sales value at the split-off point and the revenue from the by-product is credited to the cost of production.

The budget for the next period is as follows:

Processing costs: $45,000

Output in units:

Joint product X – 250 units

Joint product Y – 400 units

By-product Z – 3,000 units

Selling prices per unit: $80 for X, $100 for Y, $0.20 for Z.

The cost per unit of product Y is $_______

184 JK manufactures a product with the following standard information:

	$/unit
Direct materials	9.00
Direct labour	14.00
Total direct cost	23.00

Additional information on the product is provided as follows:

Direct labour hours per unit	2 hours
Production overhead absorption rate	$4.50 per direct labour hour
Mark-up for non-production overhead costs	10% of total production costs
Required return on sales revenue	20%

The target selling price for the product will be:

A $27.60

B $40.00

C $42.24

D $44.00

185 A factory's entire machine capacity is used to produce essential components. The costs of using the machines are as follows:

	$
Variable costs	15,000
Fixed costs	50,000
	65,000

If all of the components are purchased from an outside supplier, the machines could be used to produce other items which would earn a total contribution of $25,000.

The maximum price that a profit-maximising company should be willing to pay to the outside supplier for the components is $_______

186 The standard output from a joint process was 5,000 litres of Product K, 3,000 litres of Product L and 2,000 litres of Product M. The total cost of the joint process was $156,000. The company is now deciding if it should modify Product K by putting it through an additional process.

In order to help with that decision, the best way to apportion the joint costs of $156,000 to the products is:

A in the ratio of 5: 3: 2

B in the ratio of the sales value at the split off point

C in the ratio of the sales value after further processing

D none of the above methods

187 Which of the following costs would not be treated as a relevant cost when making a decision on a potential new contract?

A A net $2,000 saving from avoiding staff redundancies

B Extra fixed income of $600 per month

C A reduction of $4,000 in fixed supervisors' salaries

D A $4,000 expected increase in the bad debt provision

188 Which of the following is NOT a disadvantage of using a full cost pricing system?

A It cannot account for selling and distribution costs

B The final selling price is affected by arbitrary cost allocations between products

C The mark-up used is arbitrary

D Overheads will not be fully recovered if actual volume is less than budgeted volume

189 Which of the following costs is likely to be a relevant cost for decision making? (tick all that apply)

	Relevant cost?
Accounting adjustments	
Incremental fixed costs	

190 Which of the following is normally considered to be a relevant cost for decision making?

A Sunk cost

B Non-incremental cost

C Committed cost

D Opportunity cost

191 Which of the following are likely to be included when setting selling prices using marginal cost pricing? (tick all that apply)

	Included?
Prime costs	
Direct labour supervision costs	
Variable sales distribution costs	
Depreciation on factory machinery	
Selling managers' salaries	

192 A one-off project requires 60 kg of a liquid which was purchased for $12 per kg. The liquid isn't regularly used in the business and there are 40 kg in inventory. The inventory can be sold for $4 per kg and the material would cost $15 per kg to replace.

The relevant cost of using the material in the project is $_____.

193 Which TWO of the following statements regarding cost plus pricing are correct?

	Correct?
Marginal cost-plus pricing should be only used for short term decision making.	
Cost-plus pricing requires that the profit mark-up applied by an organisation is fixed.	
Cost-plus pricing is a strategically focused approach, as it accounts for external factors.	
Full cost-plus pricing requires the budgeted level of output to be determined at the outset.	

194 20 hours of skilled labour is required for a one-off project. Existing skilled staff are paid a fixed salary that is equivalent to $35 per hour. These staff are fully employed. Alternatively, the work could be outsourced to an agency who can provide equivalent skilled staff at $45 per hour.

The relevant cost for skilled labour in the project is $_______.

195 A business is considering closing one of its branches which has the following budgeted performance for the next year:

	$000
Revenue	200
Variable costs	(200)
Fixed costs	(150)
Budgeted profit (loss)	(150)

Variable costs include $50,000 for labour costs. These staff would have to be made redundant at a total cost of $20,000.

Fixed costs contain a fixed rent charge that is specific to the branch of $60,000 as well as $40,000 of centrally allocated costs. All other fixed costs will be saved if the branch is closed down.

What will be the net benefit for the year of shutting the branch?

A $0

B $90,000

C $150,000

D $170,000

196 A manufacturer produces three products in the same process which has joint process costs of $10,000. Details on the products are as follows:

Product	**Volume**	**Sales value per unit at the split off point**
X	400	$80
Y	200	$100
Z	400	$120

Joint process costs are allocated on the basis of sales value at the split off point. Product Z could be further processed for $2,000. This would increase the selling price per unit to $140.

To the nearest $, the net benefit from further processing Product Z is $_______.

197 K Limited is choosing between four options for a new office for its administration staff. Each option has been allocated a score from 1 to 100 (1 = worst, 100 = best) on three criteria.

	Criteria code	**Location A**	**Location B**	**Location C**	**Location D**
Proximity to public transport	X	100	70	50	40
On-site facilities	Y	50	60	100	70
Cost savings	Z	60	70	80	100

The decision will be made using the following weighted benefit scoring formula:

Weighted benefit score = 0.2X + 0.3Y + 0.5Z

Identify which location will be chosen based on the weighted benefit scores.

A Location A

B Location B

C Location C

D Location D

198 The following details relate to three services provided by RST Company:

	Service R	Service S	Service T
	$	$	$
Fee charged to customers	100	150	160
Unit service costs:			
Direct materials	15	30	25
Direct labour	20	35	30
Variable overhead	15	20	22
Fixed overhead	25	50	50

All three services use the same type of direct labour which is paid $25 per hour.

The fixed overheads are general fixed overheads that have been absorbed on the basis of machine hours.

If direct labour is a scarce resource, the most and least profitable uses of it are:

	Most profitable	Least profitable
A	S	R
B	S	T
C	T	R
D	T	S

199 The following details relate to ready meals that are prepared by a food processing company:

Ready meal	K $/meal	L $/meal	M $/meal
Selling price	5.00	3.00	4.40
Ingredients	2.00	1.00	1.30
Variable conversion costs	1.60	0.80	1.85
Fixed conversion costs*	0.50	0.30	0.60
Profit	0.90	0.90	0.65
Oven time (minutes per ready meal)	10	4	8

*The fixed conversion costs are general fixed costs that are not specific to any type of ready meal.

Each of the meals is prepared using a series of processes, one of which involves cooking the ingredients in a large oven. The availability of cooking time in the oven is limited and, because each of the meals requires cooking at a different oven temperature, it is not possible to cook more than one of the meals in the oven at the same time.

The most and least profitable use of the oven is: (fill in the letter for the most and least profitable meal)

	Meal?
Most profitable	
Least profitable	

200 An organisation manufactures a product with the following standard information:

	$/unit
Direct materials	9.00
Direct labour	14.00
Variable production overheads	6.00
Fixed production overheads	5.00
Total production cost	34.00

Calculate the selling price for the product if the organisation requires a profit mark-up of 25% on the marginal cost of production.

A $36.25

B $38.67

C $42.50

D $45.33

201 **Which of the following factors would be relevant in a decision about whether to close a division of an organisation? Select all that apply.**

A The effect of the decision on employee morale

B The likely reaction of customers

C The notional rent charged to the division from head office

D The effect of the decision on the organisation's public image

E The fixed costs directly attributable to the division

BREAKEVEN ANALYSIS

202 A company has budgeted breakeven sales revenue of $800,000 and fixed costs of $320,000 for the next period.

What is the sales revenue needed to achieve a profit of $50,000 in the period?

A $850,000

B $925,000

C $1,120,000

D $1,200,000

203 FPG Company sells three products – F, P and G. The ratio of their total sales values is 6F : 5P : 4G. The contribution to sales ratios of the products are:

F 35% P 20% G 30%

If fixed costs for the period are expected to be $160,000, the revenue (to the nearest $1,000) needed to earn a marginal costing profit of $40,000 is:

A $598,000

B $651,000

C $698,000

D $706,000

204 R Company provides a single service to its customers. An analysis of its budget for the year ending 31 December 20X5 shows that in period 3, when the budgeted activity was 6,570 service units with a sales value of $72 each, the margin of safety was 21.015%.

The budgeted contribution to sales ratio of the service is 35%.

Budgeted fixed costs in period 3 were nearest to:

A $115,000

B $131,000

C $145,000

D $157,000

205 **Which of the following are required to determine the breakeven sales value in a multi-product manufacturing environment?**

	Required?
The product-specific fixed costs	
The product mix ratio	
General fixed costs	
The method of apportionment of general fixed costs	
Individual product gross contribution to sales ratios	

206 R Company currently sells products S, T and U in equal quantities and at the same selling price per unit. The contribution to sales ratio for product S is 60%; for product T it is 45% and the total is 52%.

If fixed costs are unaffected by mix and are currently 25% of sales, the effect of changing the product mix to S: 45% T: 20% U: 35% is that the total contribution/total sales ratio changes to:

A 53.85%

B 52.00%

C 45.00%

D 33.33%

207 EFG Company manufactures three products, which have the following forecasts for next year:

	Product E	**Product F**	**Product G**
Sales revenue ($000)	1,200	1,500	1,900
Total contribution ($000)	360	300	475

Fixed costs are forecast to be $850,000.

The lowest breakeven sales revenue can be achieved which combination of sales:

A Product E $1,200,000; Product F $1,500,000; Product G: $760,000

B Product E $1,200,000; Product F $75,000; Product G $1,900,000

C Product E $250,000; Product F $1,500,000; Product G $1,900,000

D Product E $898,678; Product F $1,123,348; Product G $1,422,907

208 R Company manufactures and sells two products – S and T. Annual sales are expected to be in the ratio of 3S:5T. Total annual sales are planned to be $640,000. Product S has a contribution to sales ratio of 32% whereas that of product T is 48%. Annual fixed costs are estimated to be $200,000.

The margin of safety is _______% (round to one decimal place)

209 A company provides three different levels of customer service support for one of its software products. The following data relate to these three levels of support:

Support level	**Superior**	**Standard**	**Basic**
	$ per contract	$ per contract	$ per contract
Annual fee	1,000	750	400
Annual variable costs	450	250	180
Annual fixed costs (see note below)	200	100	50
Profit	350	400	170

Note The total annual fixed costs are budgeted to be $1,000,000. None of these costs are specific to any type of customer service support.

Assume that the number of customer service support contracts sold are in the proportion:

Superior 20% Standard 30% Basic 50%

The annual revenue that needs to be generated in order to break even is closest to:

A $1,690,000

B $1,695,000

C $1,710,000

D $2,270,000

210 RK Company manufactures a product that has a selling price of $14 and variable costs of $6 per unit, and incurs annual fixed costs of $24,400. Annual sales demand is 8,000 units.

A new production method is currently under consideration that would increase fixed costs by 30%, but would reduce variable costs to $5 per unit. The superior quality of the finished product would enable sales to be increased to 8,500 units per annum at a price of $15 each.

If the change in production method were to take place, what would be the impact on the breakeven output level?

A 500 units higher

B 372 units higher

C 915 units higher

D 122 units higher

211 XYZ Company sells three products.

Product X has a contribution to sales ratio of 40%.

Product Y has a contribution to sales ratio of 30%.

Product Z has a contribution to sales ratio of 35%.

Monthly fixed costs are $200,000.

The total revenue received from sales of the products is in the ratio:

X:3 Y:7 Z:5

The monthly breakeven sales revenue is $_______ (round to the nearest to $000)

212 A company has only a limited available supply of direct labour and direct materials. It manufactures two products, X and Y, for which there is unlimited sales demand at current selling prices. The resource requirements for each product are as follows:

	Product X	**Product Y**
Direct materials	2 kg	4 kg
Direct labour	3 hours	1 hour

The company seeks to maximise its profits. Each unit of product X earns a contribution of $12 per unit.

The minimum contribution that must be earned by a unit of product Y to make it worth producing units of product Y in a profit-maximising budget is $_______

213 X Company sells one product which has a contribution per unit of $10. The budgeted profit is $8,000 and fixed costs are $24,000.

What is the margin of safety, expressed a percentage of budgeted units _______%

214 A business has total costs of $50,000, 70% of which are variable. Its total revenue from its single product is $40,000.

To the nearest $000, its breakeven sales revenue is $_______.

215 S plc produces and sells three products, X, Y and Z. It has contracts to supply products X and Y, which will utilise all of the specific materials that are available to make these two products during the next period. The revenue these contracts will generate and the contribution to sales (C/S) ratios of products X and Y are as follows:

	Product X	**Product Y**
Revenue	$10 million	$20 million
C/S ratio	15%	10%

Product Z has a C/S ratio of 25%.

The total fixed costs of S plc are $5.5 million during the next period and management has budgeted to earn a profit of $2 million.

The revenue that needs to be generated by Product Z for S plc to achieve the budgeted profit is $_______ million

216 A business makes a single product. The variable cost per unit is set to increase next month.

What impact will this have on the line plotted on the budgeted Profit/Volume (P/V) chart?

A the gradient of the line will increase and the breakeven point will occur earlier

B the gradient of the line will increase and the breakeven point will occur later

C the gradient of the line will decrease and the breakeven point will occur earlier

D the gradient of the line will decrease and the breakeven point will occur later

217 If the budgeted fixed costs increase, the gradient of the line plotted on the budgeted Profit/Volume (P/V) chart will:

A increase

B decrease

C not change

D become curvi-linear

218

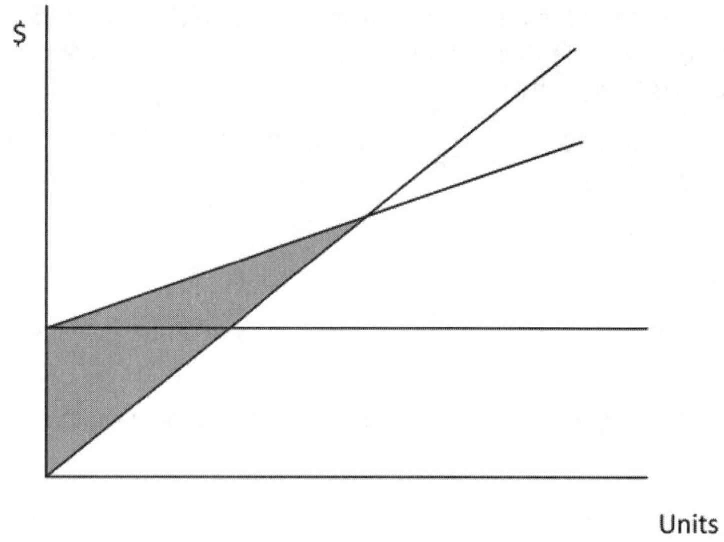

What does the shaded area on the breakeven chart above represent?

A Loss

B Fixed cost

C Variable cost

D Profit

219 A business produces a single product. Each unit has a contribution of $20. Total fixed costs are $400,000. The positive margin of safety for the product is 40% of breakeven sales units.

To the nearest $000, the budgeted profit for the product is $_______.

220 A service company provides two services with the following details

Service	**Standard**	**Advanced**
	$	$
Revenue per service	40	60
Variable costs per service	10	20
Contribution per service	30	40
Budgeted number of services	50,000	20,000

The fixed costs attached to the services are $2m.

To the nearest $000, the breakeven sales revenue for the company is $_______.

221 An organisation sells a number of products and has created the following profit volume charts:

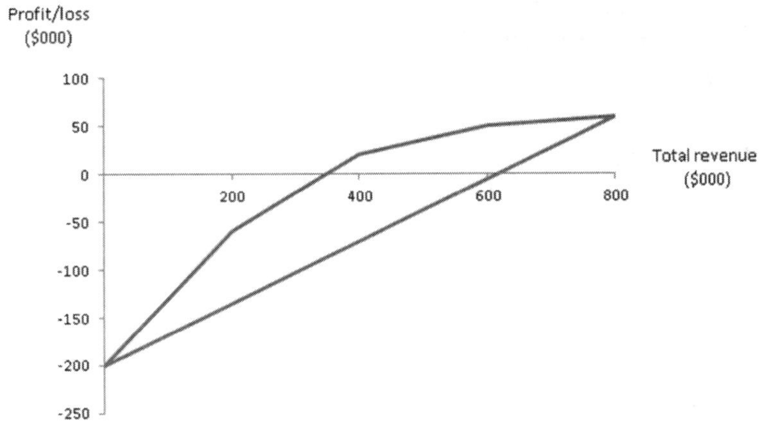

If the products are sold in the order of the most favourable contribution to sales ratio, which of the following levels of sales revenue would be closest to the organisation's breakeven point?

A $200,000

B $400,000

C $600,000

D $800,000

222 Which of the following is not normally an assumption when determining the breakeven point in a multi-product environment?

A The sales mix for the products remains constant

B Products are sold in order of their contribution sales ratio

C Contribution per unit for each product doesn't change

D Semi-variable costs can be split into their variable and fixed components

223 A safety training school provides two courses with details as follows:

Product	**Compulsory**	**Optional**
Percentage of budgeted sales revenue	70%	30%
Contribution to sales ratio	75%	80%

Combined fixed costs are $22,000.

To the nearest $000, the total breakeven sales revenue for the products is $_______.

224 A company manufactures and sells a single product, XY for $56 per unit. In March, budgeted volume was 7,200 units, the margin of safety was 26.2%. The budgeted contribution to sales ratio is 21%.

What are the budgeted fixed costs for March?

A $106,856

B $62,493

C $84,672

D $105,638

225

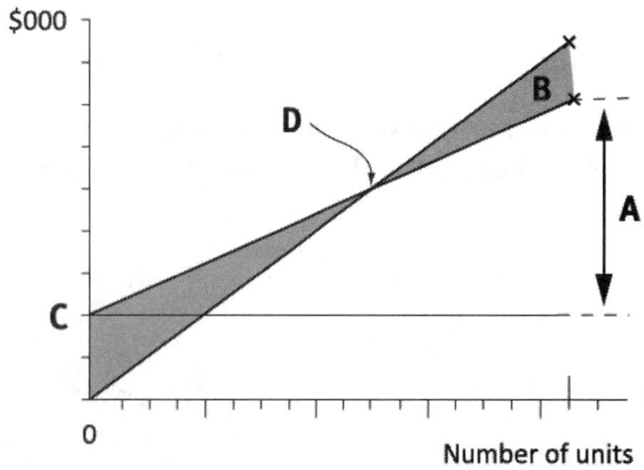

What does A represent on the above breakeven chart?

A Fixed costs

B Variable costs

C Contribution

D Profit

226 An organisation manufactures and sells three different products, with the following budgeted information for the next period:

	Product X	Product Y	Product Z
Revenue	$10 million	$15 million	$20 million
C/S ratio	9%	15%	25%

A profit-volume chart has been prepared based on expected levels of demand in the next period. However, due to a recent economic downturn, it is expected that a large proportion of customers will now switch from Product Z to Product X. The total level of sales and the remainder of the cost estimates for the period are not expected to change.

If this prediction is correct, which TWO of the following statements are true?

A The overall gradient of the weighted average line on the profit-volume line will become steeper

B The margin of safety will reduce

C The starting point of the line will stay the same

D The breakeven point will not change

LINEAR PROGRAMMING

227 A linear programming model has been formulated with the following objective function:

Objective function Max 4X + 2Y

The optimal solution has determined that 400 X and 600 Y should be produced. An extra litre of materials would, however, change this to 400.5 X and 599.5 Y. Materials cost $9 per litre.

To the nearest $, the shadow price per litre for materials is $_______.

228 **Which ONE of the following statements is NOT true?**

A Linear programming techniques should not be used when there is only one scarce resource

B Linear programming assumes that products must be made in full units

C Linear programming aims to maximise contribution to profits

D Linear programming techniques can cope with more than two scarce resources at the same time

229 An organisation is preparing a linear programming model. The company makes two products, X and Y. It needs to produce twice as many Y than X.

In the linear programming model, X will be used to represent the number of units of Product X produced and Y will be used to represent the number of units of Product Y produced.

Which ONE of the following represents the correct constraint for the production of the products?

A $2X \geq Y$

B $X \geq 2Y$

C $X = 2Y$

D $2X = Y$

230 A company manufactures two products with the following details:

	Ultra	**Maxi**
	$	$
Selling price	60	85
Materials (@ $4 per kg)	16	12
Labour (@ $20 per hour)	20	40
	–––	–––
Contribution	24	33
	–––	–––

Material is a scarce resource and has a shadow price of $2 per kg. A new supplier has offered to supply extra materials but at a premium price.

The highest acceptable price per kg for the extra materials is $_______.

231 An organisation has the following contribution function:

Contribution = 6A + 4B

where

A = the number of units of product A produced, and

B = the number of units of product B produced.

A graph has identified that the optimal production plan exists at the point where the following two constraints cross:

Material X: A + 2B ≤ 9,000

Material Y: 3A + B ≤ 12,000

There is a maximum demand of 10,000 units of each product.

How many units of Product A are produced in order to maximise contribution?

A 0

B 3,000

C 9,000

D 15,000

232 An organisation is preparing a linear programming model. Its production process needs two types of labour, skilled and unskilled. There are only 4,000 hours of each available.

Usage per unit of the two types of labour for the organisation's two products is as follows:

	Skilled labour	**Unskilled labour**
Product A	5 hours	5 hours
Product B	1 hour	1 hour

In the linear programming model, X will be used to represent the number of units of Product A produced and Y will be used to represent the number of units of Product B produced.

Which ONE of the following represents the correct constraint for unskilled labour?

A 5X + 1Y ≤ 4,000

B 5X + 5Y ≤ 4,000

C 1X + 5Y ≤ 4,000

D 1X + 1Y ≤ 4,000

233 **The shadow price of skilled labour for CBV Limited is currently $8 per hour. What does this mean?**

A The cost of obtaining additional skilled labour resources is $8 per hour

B There is a hidden cost of $8 for each hour of skilled labour actively worked

C Contribution will be increased by $8 per hour for each extra hour of skilled labour that can be obtained

D Total costs will be reduced by $8 for each additional hour of skilled labour that can be obtained

234 Q plc makes two products – A and B – from the same raw material. The selling price and cost details of these products are as shown below:

	A	B
	$	$
Selling price	20.00	18.00
Direct material ($2.00 per kg)	6.00	5.00
Direct labour	4.00	3.00
Variable overhead	2.00	1.50
Contribution per unit	8.00	8.50
Maximum weekly demand	500 units	Unlimited

If material were limited to 2,000 kgs per week, the shadow price of these materials would be:

A $nil

B $2.00 per kg

C $2.66 per kg

D $3.40 per kg

235 A company products two products, X and Y and is determining its production plan for the year ahead.

Details of the two products are as follows:

	Product X	Product Y
	$	$
Selling price	50.00	80.00
Direct material ($5.00 per kg)	15.00	20.00
Direct labour ($10 per hour)	20.00	35.00
Contribution per unit	15.00	25.00

The company's objective is to maximise contribution. Linear programming has been used to determine the optimum production plan is where the following constraints intersect:

Materials: $2X + 6Y \leq 1{,}700$

Machine hours: $4X + 8Y \leq 2{,}500$

The maximum contribution which can be earned from these two products is $_______

236 Company XY manufactures two products, Product X and Product Y.

The company's objective is to maximise contribution. However, production is restricted by the following constraints.

Materials: $4X + 6Y \leq 2{,}000$

Labour: $4X + 8Y \leq 2{,}500$

Machine hours: $3X + 5Y \leq 1{,}800$

Linear programming has been used to determine the optimum production is where the materials and labour constraints intersect.

If the optimum production plan is applied, the number of spare machine hours available (slack) will be_______

237 An organisation has created the following linear programming solution to represent the position it faces currently in the presence of short term scarce resources:

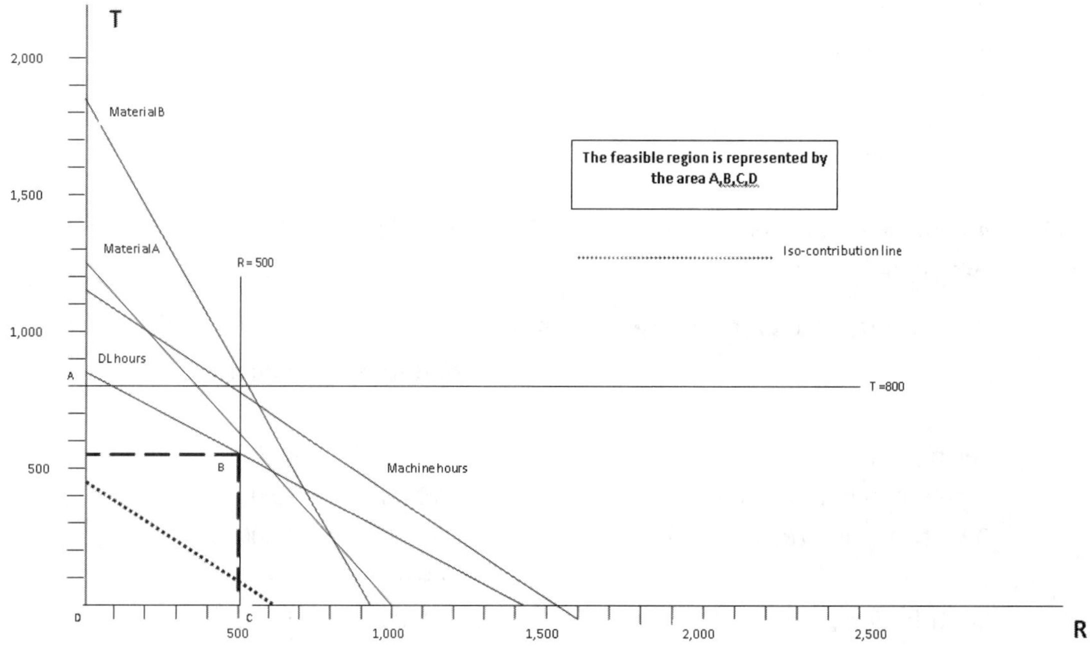

Note: DL = Direct labour hours

The point marked B has been determined to be the point which provides the optimal production plan.

Which of the following resources will have a shadow price greater than 0? (tick all that apply)

	Shadow price > 0?
Direct labour hours	
Material A	
Material B	
Machine hours	

238 Which of the following are limitations of the linear programming technique?

	Limitation?
Linear relationships must exist	
There can only be two products	
There can only be two scarce resources	
All variables must be completely divisible	
A computer must be used to find the optimal point	

239 JRL manufactures two products from different combinations of the same resources. Unit selling prices and unit cost details for each product are as follows:

Product	**J**	**L**
	$/unit	$/unit
Selling price	115	120
Direct material A ($10 per kg)	20	10
Direct material B ($6 per kg)	12	24
Skilled labour ($14 per hour)	28	21
Variable overhead ($4 per machine hour)	14	18
Fixed overhead	28	36

Which of the following equations represents the iso-contribution line?

A 13J + 11L = M

B 41J + 47L = M

C 54J + 58L = M

D 54J + 65L = M

240 An organisation has the following contribution function:

Contribution = 5X + 10Y

where

X = the number of units of product X produced, and

Y = the number of units of product Y produced.

A graph has identified that the optimal production plan exists at the point where the following two constraints cross:

Skilled labour: 6X + 4Y ≤ 62,000

Unskilled labour: 2X + 5Y ≤ 50,000

There is a maximum demand of 12,000 units of each product.

The number of units of Product Y produced in order to maximise contribution (to the nearest whole unit) is _______ units.

241 An organization has created the following linear programming solution to represent the position it faces currently in the presence of short term scarce resources:

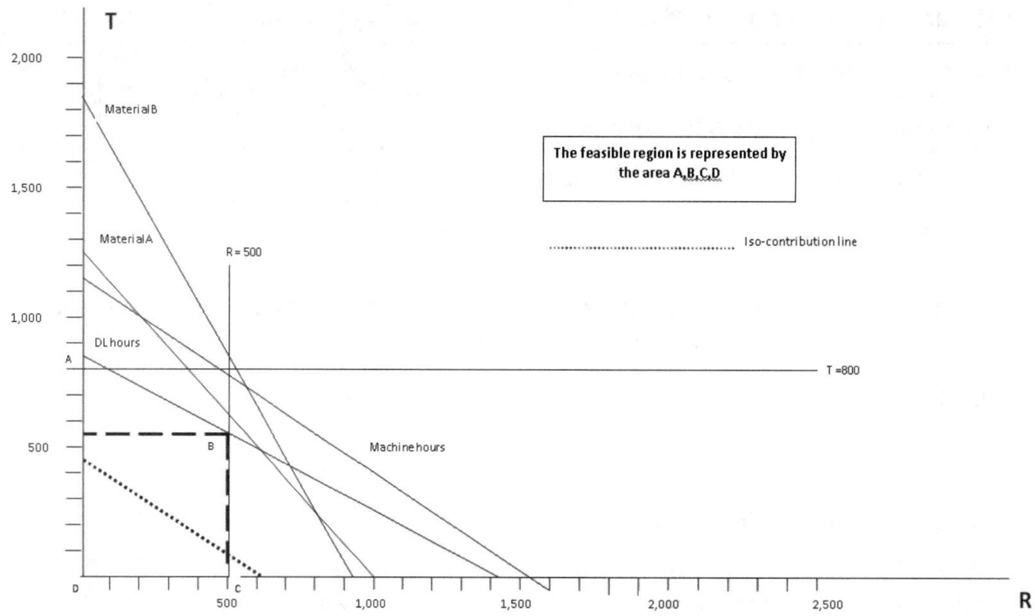

The organisation manufactures two products, T and R. Each T requires 1.6 kgs of material A and each R requires 2 kgs of material A.

The maximum amount of Material A available is _______ kgs

242 An organisation has the following contribution function:

Contribution = 12A + 8B, where

A = the number of units of product A produced, and

B = the number of units of product B produced.

A graph has identified that the optimal production plan exists at the point where the following two constraints cross:

Material X: A + 2B ≤ 8,000

Material Y: 2A + B ≤ 13,000

There is a maximum demand of 10,000 units of each product.

How many units of Product A are produced in order to maximise contribution?

A 0

B 1,000

C 6,000

D 10,000

243 An organisation has graphed the following linear programming model:

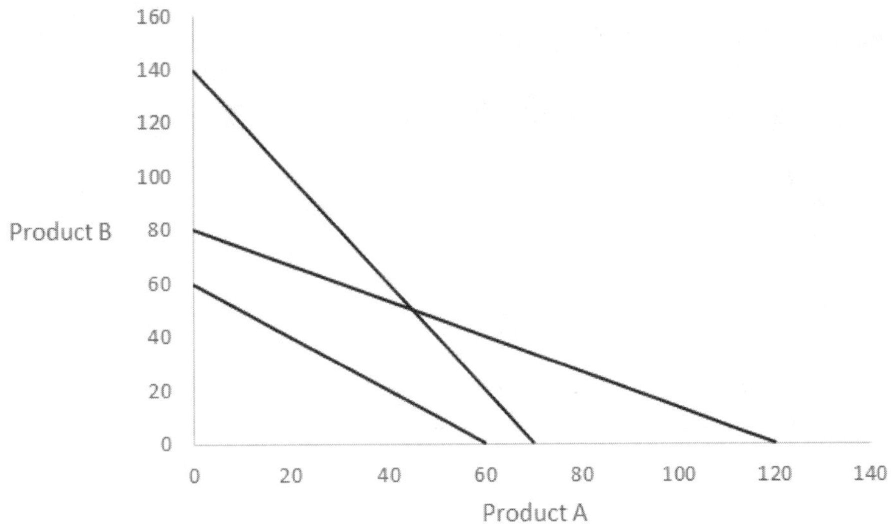

All constraints have less than or equal to limits.

The maximum number of units of Product B which can be produced is _______ units.

244 Which TWO of the following statements related to linear programming are correct?

A Linear programming can only be used for profit maximisation problems

B Slack occurs when the maximum availability of a resource is not fully used at the optimal solution point

C Binding constraints will always have a shadow price

D Linear programming can be applied to organisations with multiple objectives

245 Which of the following are advantages of using spreadsheets for linear programming?

(i) Spreadsheets can identify data input errors.

(ii) Spreadsheets can produce graphs to assist analysis and reporting.

(iii) Using spreadsheet formula enables the input data to be altered quickly.

(iv) Using spreadsheets should reduce calculation errors.

A (i), (ii) and (iii)

B (ii), (iii) and (iv)

C (i), (iii) and (iv)

D (i) and (ii) only

RISK AND UNCERTAINTY IN THE SHORT TERM

RISK AND UNCERTAINTY IN THE SHORT TERM

246 The daily demand for a perishable product has the following probability distribution:

Demand (units)	Probability
100	0.25
200	0.40
300	0.35

Each item costs $4 and is sold for $8. Unsold items are thrown away at the end of the day.

If orders must be placed before the daily demand is known, the number of units that should be purchased at the beginning of each day in order to maximise expected profit is _______ units

247 A company has estimated the selling prices and variable costs of one of its products as follows:

Selling price per unit		Variable cost per unit	
$	Probability	$	Probability
40	0.30	20	0.55
50	0.45	30	0.25
60	0.25	40	0.20

The company will be able to supply 1,000 units of its product each week irrespective of the selling price. Selling price and variable cost per unit are independent of each other.

The probability that the weekly contribution will exceed $20,000 is _______% (round to the nearest whole %)

248 X Company can choose from five mutually exclusive projects. The projects will each last for one year only and their net cash inflows will be determined by the prevailing market conditions. The forecast annual cash inflows and their associated probabilities are shown below:

Market conditions	Poor	Good	Excellent
Probability	0.20	0.50	0.30
	$000	$000	$000
Project L	500	470	550
Project M	400	550	570
Project N	450	400	475
Project O	360	400	420
Project P	600	500	425

Based on the expected value of the net cash inflows, which project should be undertaken?

A L

B M

C N

D P

249 A baker is trying to decide the number of batches of a particular type of bread that they should bake each day. Daily demand ranges from 10 batches to 12 batches and the daily contribution from each combination of supply and demand is outlined in the table below.

Contribution table		**Batches baked**		
		10	11	12
	10	500	480	460
Daily demand	11	500	550	530
	12	500	550	600

Assuming the baker adopts the minimax regret decision rule, the number of batches of bread that they should bake each day is _______ batches

250 **Match the decision criterion with the assumed approach to risk taken by the decision maker (draw a line connecting the decision criteria to the correct attitude to risk)**

Decision criteria
Expected values
Maximax
Maximin
Minimax regret

Attitude to risk
Risk averse
Risk averse
Riske neutral
Risk seeker

251 A company is making a decision on whether to launch a new product. The decision is illustrated in the following decision tree:

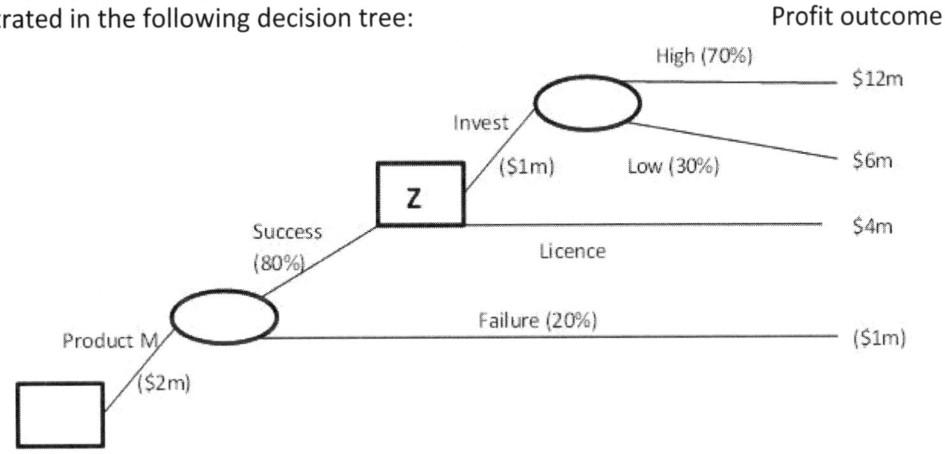

The profit outcomes do not include the cost of any investments made.

The expected value at point Z is $9.2m.

What is the overall expected value from the product launch?

A $5.16m

B $7.16m

C $7.36m

D $9.20m

252 On investigating the labour efficiency variance an organisation has found that there is typically a favourable variance of mean of $60,000 and a standard deviation of $5,000.

The probability that the variance is less than $45,000 is _____% (answer to two decimal places)

253 A florist orders bunches of flowers from a wholesaler which are then sold on a market stall. Flowers have to ordered before the demand is known; any unsold flowers are thrown away at the end of the day.

A payoff table below shows the expected profits based upon the quantity ordered and the level of demand.

	Order level (supply)			
Demand	20 bunches	30 bunches	40 bunches	50 bunches
20 bunches	$60	$20	$(20)	$(60)
30 bunches	$60	$90	$50	$10
40 bunches	$60	$90	$120	$80
50 bunches	$60	$90	$120	$150

Using a minimax regret table, the order level that would be selected if the florist applies the minimax regret decision criterion is:

A 20 bunches

B 30 bunches

C 40 bunches

D 50 bunches

254 A chocolate manufacturer has to decide which of three new chocolate bars to launch. Demand is uncertain and could occur at one of three levels: low, medium or high. The management accountant uses expected values to make this type of decision and this has resulted in predicted expected profit of $142,000.

The market is highly competitive and so the manufacturer has decided to employ the services of a market research company who can provide perfect information about the likely demand level.

The manufacturer is prepared to pay a maximum of $15,000 for the information from the market research company.

Calculate the value of the expected profit with this information.

A $157,000

B $127,000

C $112,000

D $97,000

255 **Perfect information is described as:**

A 100% accurate

B 85% accurate

C Sometimes accurate

D Never accurate

256 P Company currently sells 90,000 units of product Y per annum. At this level of sales and output, the selling price and variable cost per unit are $50 and $21 respectively. The annual fixed costs are $1,200,000. The management team is considering lowering the selling price per unit to $45.

The estimated levels of demand at the new price, and the probabilities of them occurring, are:

Selling price of $45

Demand	**Probability**
100,000 units	0.45
120,000 units	0.55

It is thought that at either of the higher sales and production levels, the variable cost per unit, and the probability of it occurring, will be as follows:

Variable cost (per unit)	**Probability**
$20	0.40
$18	0.60

The probability that lowering the selling price to $45 per unit would increase profit is _______% (round to the nearest whole %)

257 A company expects to sell 1,000 units per month of a new product but there is uncertainty as to both the unit selling price and the unit variable cost of the product. The following estimates of selling price, variable costs and their related probabilities have been made:

Selling price		**Unit variable cost**	
$ per unit	Probability	$ per unit	Probability
20	25%	8	20%
25	40%	10	50%
30	35%	12	30%

There are specific fixed costs of $5,000 per month expected for the new product.

What is the expected value of monthly contribution?

A $5,890

B $10,300

C $10,890

D $15,300

258 **Which of the following are disadvantages of using an expected value technique?**

	Disadvantage of EVs?
Expected values only provides the most likely result	
It ignores attitudes to risk	
Only two possible outcomes can be considered	
Probabilities are subjective	
The answer provided may not exist	

259 The committee of a new golf club is setting the annual membership fee. The number of members depends on the membership fee charged and economic conditions. The forecast annual cash inflows from membership fees are shown below.

Membership fee	Membership level		
	Low	Average	High
	$000	$000	$000
$600	360	480	540
$800	400	440	480
$900	360	405	495
$1,000	320	380	420

What would be the fee set by the committee if the maximin criterion is applied?

A $600

B $800

C $900

D $1,000

260 A cafe owner is trying to decide how many cakes he/she/they should bake each day. The demand is uncertain and he/she/they have to make the cakes at the start of each day before the demand level is known.

The payoff table below shows the daily contribution that can be expected depending on the number of cakes baked and the level of demand that occurs.

	Number of cakes baked		
Level of demand	20	25	30
Low	$14	$11.5	$9
Medium	$14	$17.5	$15
High	$14	$17.5	$21

The number of cakes that should be baked if the maximax decision criterion is applied is _____

261 X Company can choose from five mutually exclusive projects. The projects will each last for one year only and their net cash inflows will be determined by the prevailing market conditions. The forecast annual cash inflows and their associated probabilities are shown below:

Market conditions	**Poor**	**Good**	**Excellent**	**Expected**
Probability	0.20	0.50	0.30	**value**
	$000	$000	$000	$000
Project L	500	470	550	500
Project M	400	550	570	526
Project N	450	400	475	432.5
Project O	360	400	420	398
Project P	600	500	425	497.6

What would be the value of perfect information about the state of the market?

A Nil

B $5,000

C $26,000

D $40,000

262 A company is trying to decide which of four products it should launch. The demand is uncertain and is based on optimistic, likely and pessimistic forecasts. A regret matrix has been prepared showing the regret for each of the outcomes depending on the decision made.

Regret matrix	**Product**			
Demand forecast	W	X	Y	Z
Optimistic	$43,000	$0	$73,000	$38,000
Likely	$15,000	$5,000	$35,000	$0
Pessimistic	$0	$17,000	$42,000	$25,000

If the company applies the minimax regret criterion to make decisions, which product would be chosen?

A W

B X

C Y

D Z

263 A company is considering launching one of two new products. If the product is successful in its first month there will be an opportunity to either make a further investment, or to licence all future development to another company. The decision for the company is illustrated by the following decision tree:

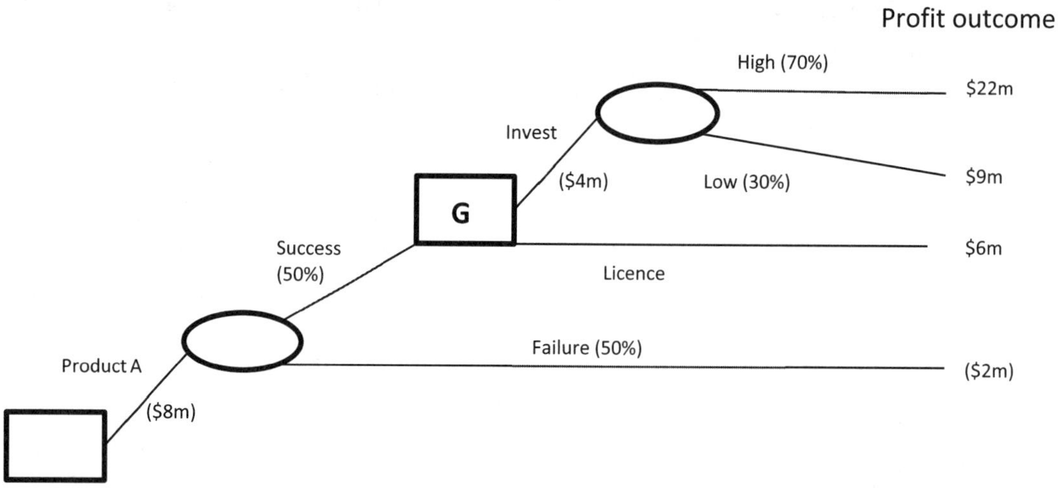

The profit outcomes do not include the cost of any investments made.

What is the expected value at point G?

A $6m

B $14.1m

C $18.1m

D $20.1m

264 A toy retailer is considering introducing a new product and has to decide if the sales price should be $100, $105, $110 or $115. There is a 30% chance that demand could be high, a 50% chance that demand will be at a medium level and a 20% chance that demand will be low.

A payoff table below shows the profits based upon the sales price and the level of demand.

	Sales price			
Demand	$100	$105	$110	$115
High	$1,700,000	$1,725,000	$1,700,000	$1,625,000
Medium	$700,000	$600,000	$450,000	$250,000
Low	$100,000	$60,000	$0	$(80,000)

The retailer has decided, using an expected value approach, the sales price should be set at $100 as this gives the highest expected profit of $880,000.

A market research company has since approached the retailer and it believes it can provide perfect information on the demand level.

The maximum amount that should be paid for the information from the market research company is $_______ (Answer should be given to the nearest whole $)

265 S Ltd makes paddling pools and has to decide in advance how many pools to make before the summer demand is known. Demand is determined by the weather, if it is very hot and sunny demand will be high, if it is a rainy cold summer demand will be low and a warm summer will result in average demand.

The budgeted profit for the current year is $1,190,000. The profit for the previous year was very low due to a wet summer so S Ltd is considering employing the services of a meteorologist to predict the likely weather for this summer. The predictions are not perfect but should give a good indication.

S Ltd has decided that it is prepared to pay a maximum of $30,000 for the meteorologist services as using the predictions should result in an expected profit of $1,250,000.

What is the expected profit for S Ltd if the meteorologist had not been employed?

A $1,280,000

B $1,250,000

C $1,220,000

D $1,190,000

266 A national chain of coffee shops has three potential new sites available:

		SHOP SIZE (supply)		
Demand	**Probability**	**Small**	**Medium**	**Large**
Strong	0.2	354,600	894,300	1,413,200
Good	0.4	172,100	529,300	865,700
Weak	0.4	80,850	255,550	226,950

If the management team used an expected value approach, it would have decided to open a large shop as this gives the highest expected value of $719,700.

A market research company believes it can provide perfect information on the potential demand level.

The maximum amount that should be paid for the information from the market research company is $_______ (Answer should be given to the nearest whole $)

267 A café owner is trying to decide how many cakes he/she/they should bake each day. The demand is uncertain and the owner has to make the cakes at the start of each day before the demand level is known.

The payoff table below shows the daily contribution that can be expected depending on the number of cakes baked and the level of demand that occurs.

	Number of cakes baked		
Level of demand	20	25	30
Low	$14	$11.5	$9
Medium	$14	$17.5	$15
High	$14	$17.5	$21

The number of cakes that should baked if the maximin decision criterion is applied is _____

268 The committee of a new golf club is setting the annual membership fee. The number of members depends on the membership fee charged and economic conditions. The forecast annual cash inflows from membership fees are shown below.

Membership fee	Membership level		
	Low	**Average**	**High**
	$000	$000	$000
$600	360	480	540
$800	400	440	480
$900	360	405	495
$1,000	320	380	420

What would be the fee set by the committee if the minimax regret criterion is applied?

A $600

B $800

C $900

D $1,000

269 P Company currently sells 90,000 units of product Y per annum. At this level of sales and output, the selling price and variable cost per unit are $50 and $21 respectively. The annual fixed costs are $1,200,000. The management team is considering lowering the selling price per unit to $45.

The estimated levels of demand at the new price, and the probabilities of them occurring, are:

Selling price of $45

Demand	**Probability**
100,000 units	0.45
120,000 units	0.55

It is thought that at either of the higher sales and production levels, the variable cost per unit, and the probability of it occurring, will be as follows:

Variable cost (per unit)	**Probability**
$20	0.40
$18	0.60

The expected value of the company profit if the selling price is reduced to $45 per unit is $_______

270 A company is considering launching one of two new products. If the product is successful in its first month there will be an opportunity to either make a further investment, or to outsource all future development to another company. The decision for the company is illustrated by the following decision tree:

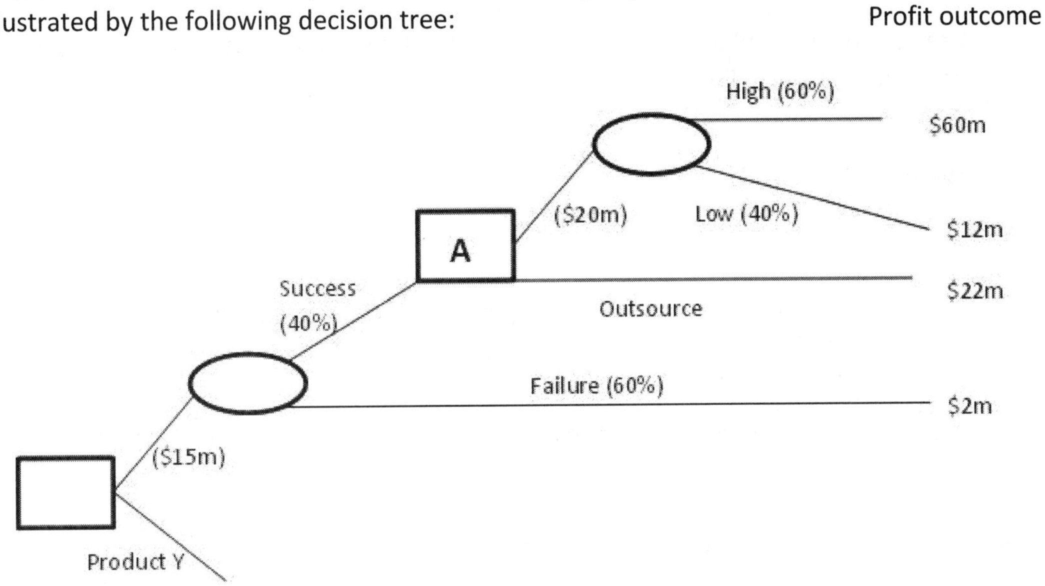

The profit outcomes do not include the cost of any investments made.

The expected value at point A on the decision trees (to the nearest $0.1m) is $_____m

271 A company expects to sell 1,000 units per month of a new product but there is uncertainty as to both the unit selling price and the unit variable cost of the product. The following estimates of selling price, variable costs and their related probabilities have been made:

Selling price		**Unit variable cost**	
$ per unit	Probability	$ per unit	Probability
20	25%	8	20%
25	40%	10	50%
30	35%	12	30%

There are specific fixed costs of $5,000 per month expected for the new product.

What is the probability of monthly contribution from this new product exceeding $13,500?

A 24.5%

B 30.5%

C 63.0%

D 92.5%

272 A theatre has a seating capacity of 500 people and is considering hiring an orchestra for a concert for one night only. The fee payable to the orchestra would be $10,000. If the theatre hires the orchestra, then this sum is payable regardless of the size of the theatre audience.

The size of the audience for this event is uncertain, but based on past experience it is expected to be as follows:

	Probability
300 people	50%
400 people	30%
500 people	20%

There is also some uncertainty regarding the contribution made from the sale of each theatre ticket. It is thought that there is a 70% chance that this would be $25 per person and a 30% chance that it would be $40 per person.

Using expected values, the financial benefit from hiring the orchestra for the concert is $_____

273 **Which TWO of the following statements are true?**

	True?
As standard deviation increases risk increases	
Imperfect information cannot be 100% correct	
A risk seeking investor typically focuses on expected values	
Expected value calculations consider the range of possible outcomes	
A variable with a smaller coefficient of variation is less risky	

274 A coffee shop is considering launching a new home delivery service. The manager has identified two possible outcomes of the decision

Outcome	**Probability**	**Profit/(Loss)**
Good	0.7	$24,000
Poor	0.3	($8,000)

What percentage increase in the loss would change the manager's decision?

A 56%

B 169%

C 300%

D 600%

275 Which ONE of the following describes a project which a risk-seeking individual is likely to pursue?

A The project with the best of the worst outcomes, regardless of probability

B The project with the highest expected value

C The project which includes the most likely outcome

D The project with the highest outcome, regardless of probability

276 Which TWO of the following statements about expected values are not correct?

(i) The expected value will always correspond to one of the possible outcomes

(ii) The expected value takes risk into account

(iii) The expected value gives no indication of the dispersion of the possible outcomes

(iv) The expected value is most suited to one-off decisions

A Statements (i) and (ii)

B Statements (ii) and (iii)

C Statements (i) and (iv)

D Statements (i) and (iii)

277 A risk averse individual is considering which one of three mutually exclusive projects to invest in. Summarised information about the projects is provided below:

Project	EV of return $	Standard deviation
1	4,300	550
2	1,800	380
3	6,300	600

Based on the above information, the individual is likely to invest in Project: [ ]

Section 2

ANSWERS TO OBJECTIVE TEST QUESTIONS

COST ACCOUNTING FOR DECISION AND CONTROL

RATIONALES FOR COSTING

1 B

Reporting is the main purpose of financial accounting. The main purposes of management accounting are planning, control and decision making.

2

	Management accounting	**Financial accounting**
Uses only historical data		✓
Is carried out at the discretion of management	✓	
Uses non-financial information	✓	
Aids planning within the organisation	✓	

3

	Strategic?
Making day-to-day decisions about the running of a department	
Defining the objectives of the company	✓
Deciding in which markets to operate	✓
Deciding about how to compete within their chosen markets	
Inventory control	

Strategic level management would normally define the objectives of the company and make decisions about which markets to operate in. Tactical level managers would then decide how best to operate in these markets while operational level managers would make day-to-day decisions required in running their departments such as inventory control.

4 B

Direct costs are those costs which can be economically identified with a single cost unit.

5 D

Although total fixed costs are the same at all levels of activity, the fixed cost per unit falls as the activity level increases. The unit cost does not fall in a straight line, but in a curve as shown in the question.

6 B

Managers are not usually classified as direct labour, because their salary cost cannot be traced to specific cost units.

7 C

High Low Method	**Activity**	$	
	6,500	33,000	
	4,500	29,000	
Difference	2,000	4,000	
So the variable cost	= $4,000/2,000	= $2 per unit	
Substitute into either activity	6,500	33,000	Total cost
	6,500 × $2	13,000	Variable cost
	Difference	$20,000	Fixed cost

The estimated production cost for 5,750 units = 5,750 × $2 + $20,000 = $31,500

8 The total fixed costs for a budgeted output of 36,000 units are $86,000

It is known that there is a stepped fixed cost of $10,000 above 35,000 units. Removing the stepped fixed cost at 40,000 units leaves $184,000.

(i)

$$\text{Variable cost per unit} = \frac{\$184{,}000 - \$143{,}500}{40{,}000 - 25{,}000} = \$2.70$$

(ii) At 25,000 units

Total cost	143,500
Total variable cost $2.70 × 25,000	67,500
Fixed cost	76,000

Therefore, fixed cost at 36,000 units = $76,000 + $10,000 = $86,000

9 C

	Machine hours	$
High	12,212	39,477
Low	8,480	31,080
Change	3,732	8,397

Variable cost per machine hour	=	$8,397/3,732
	=	$2.25
Fixed cost = $39,477 – (12,212 × $2.25)	=	$12,000

Budget cost allowance for 9,340 machine hours:

		$
Fixed cost		12,000
Variable cost (9,340 × $2.25)	=	21,015
		33,015

10 C

Cost before stepped increase = $2,840,000 – $30,000 = $2,810,000

Variable cost per unit = ($2,810,000 – $2,420,000)/ (190,000 – 160,000)

= $390,000/30,000 = $13

Fixed costs at 190,000 units = $2,840,000 – (190,000 × $13)

= $370,000

Total costs at 175,000 units = (175,000 × $13) + ($370,000 – $30,000)

= $2,615,000

11 D

The organisation is looking to control its overhead costs. In order to control them, the organisation first needs to understand what causes/drives the overheads. Switching to an activity-based costing system would highlight why the costs change and how different variables impact on the cost, so that plans can then be put in place to reduce the cost drivers.

TRADITIONAL COSTING

12 B

	$
Marginal costing profit	45,000
Less: fixed cost included in opening inventory (28,000 – 16,000)	(12,000)
Plus: fixed cost included in closing inventory (36,400 – 20,800)	15,600
Absorption costing profit	48,600

Alternative approach

Increase in inventory using marginal costing	$4,800
Increase in inventory using absorption costing	$8,400
Difference = fixed overhead absorbed in inventory	$3,600

Inventory is increasing so absorption costing profit is higher than marginal costing profit by the amount of fixed overhead absorbed.

Absorption costing profit = $45,000 + $3,600 = $48,600

13 B

The opening inventory was 400 units and the closing inventory was 900 units, therefore inventory has increased.

If production is greater than sales, then absorption costing will show the higher profit.

Difference in profit: = Change in inventory × Fixed production cost per unit

= (900 – 400) × $29,500/5,000 units = $2,950

14 A

OAR = $330,000/220,000 = $1.50 per unit

	$
Overhead absorbed (200,000 units × $1.50)	300,000
Actual overhead	260,000
Over absorbed	40,000

15 The profit for the period using absorption costing is $7,170

Value of closing inventory =$(13,500 + 11,800 + 32,400) × 200/2,000 = $5,770

	$	$
Sales (1,800 × $45)		81,000
Cost of production	57,700	
Less closing inventory	5,770	
Cost of sales		51,930
Gross profit		29,070
Non-production overhead		21,900
Profit		7,170

16 D

		Correct?
(i)	A cost driver is any factor that causes a change in the cost of an activity.	✓
(ii)	For long-term variable overhead costs, the cost driver will be the volume of activity.	✓
(iii)	Traditional absorption costing tends to under-allocate overhead costs to low-volume products.	✓

Statement (i) provides a definition of a cost driver. Cost drivers for long-term variable overhead costs will be the volume of a particular activity to which the cost driver relates, so Statement (ii) is correct. Statement (iii) is also correct. In traditional absorption costing, standard high-volume products receive a higher amount of overhead costs than with ABC. ABC allows for the unusually high costs of support activities for low-volume products (such as relatively higher set-up costs, order processing costs and so on).

17 **The profit for the period using marginal costing is $233,394.**

Variable costs of production per unit = $(126,500 + 76,800) / 5,000 units = $40.66 per unit.

Value of closing inventory = $40.66 × 900 units = $36,594

	$	$
Sales		492,000
Variable cost of production	203,300	
Less closing inventory	36,594	
Cost of sales		166,706
Contribution		325,294
Fixed overhead (68,000 + 23,900)		91,900
Profit		233,394

Alternative solution

Profit = total contribution less fixed costs

Total contribution = $(120 – 40.66) × 4,100 units = $325,294

Profit = $325,294 – $91,900 = $233,394

18 **A**

	$
Actual overhead incurred	481,250
Less under-absorbed overhead	19,250
Overhead absorbed	462,000

Overhead absorbed = Actual standard hours charged × OAR

So OAR = overhead absorbed/actual standard hours charged = $462,000/38,500 = $12

OAR = Budgeted overheads/budgeted labour hours

So budgeted overheads = OAR × budgeted labour hours = $12 × 38,000 = $456,000

19 **B**

OAR = $500,000/2,000 = $250 per unit

Inventory has fallen by 300 units in the period.

Absorption costing profit will be 300 × $250 = $75,000 lower than marginal costing profit as some fixed overhead from previous periods will be brought forward to be matched against sales in the period using absorption costing. In marginal costing only the fixed overhead incurred in the period will be included in the profit statement.

20 C

Option A may lead to over-absorption but this will depend on the extent to which actual overhead costs differ from budget. Option B describes under-absorption. Option D refers to budgeted overheads, which are used to calculate the OAR but otherwise not used in the calculation of under-/over-absorption.

21 The under-absorption of fixed production overheads for the assembly department is $480.

OAR for assembly department = $149,600/100,000 = $1.496 per unit

	$
Overhead absorbed 120,000 × 1.496	179,520
Overhead incurred	180,000
Under-absorption	480

22 A

	$000	$000
Sales revenue		820
Variable cost of sales		
Variable production costs	300	
Less: closing inventory	45	255
Variable selling costs		105
Contribution		460
Fixed costs		
Production	180	
Selling	110	290
Profit		170

Working

The closing inventory is valued at cost. As it is a marginal costing system the inventory is valued at variable cost, i.e. $300,000/1,000 units = $300 per unit. The closing inventory is 150 units therefore the closing inventory value is $300/unit × 150 units = $45,000.

23 **The total gross profit for the deluxe speedboat using absorption costing is $16,800.**

Fixed production overheads = $69,600,000

Budgeted machine hours = (1,000 × 100) + (1,200 × 200) + (800 × 300) = 580,000

Fixed production overhead absorption rate = $69,600,000/580,000 = $120 per machine hour

	Deluxe
	$000
Sales	86,400
Direct material	27,400
Direct labour	13,400
Production overhead	28,800
Gross profit	16,800

24 **D**

Statement D is correct. Profits can be manipulated by changes in inventory levels. For example, by increasing output, more fixed production overhead is absorbed into production costs, and if the extra output is not sold then this fixed production overhead cost will be carried forward in the closing inventory value. This can encourage managers to over-produce in order to inflate profits in the current year.

Statement A is referring to overhead apportionment and is therefore incorrect.

Statement B is incorrect. Whilst number of units, machine hours or labour are the most common bases, they are not the only methods that an organisation may use.

Statement C is incorrect. Overhead absorption rates are calculated at the beginning of a period using budgeted figures.

25 **B, D**

Statement A is an advantage of absorption costing, not marginal.

Statement C is incorrect. Marginal costing is useful for short-term decision-making, but not for measuring costs and profitability over the longer term.

ACTIVITY BASED COSTING

26

		Facility-sustaining	**Product-sustaining**
(i)	General staff administration	✓	
(ii)	Plant management	✓	
(iii)	Technical support for individual products and services		✓
(iv)	Updating of product specification database		✓
(v)	Property management	✓	

27 A

$$\text{Cost driver rate} = \frac{\text{Budgeted cost of orders}}{\text{Budgeted number of orders}} = \frac{\$110{,}010}{2{,}895} = \$38 \text{ per order}$$

	$
Cost recovered: 210 orders × $38	7,980
Actual costs incurred	7,650
Over-recovery of costs for four-week period	330

28 The cost per unit attributed to product R for machine set ups is $0.52

Machine set up costs for Product R

Budgeted machine set-ups:

Product D (1,000 × 3)	=	3,000
Product R (2,000 × 4)	=	8,000
Product P (2,000 × 6)	=	12,000
		23,000

$$\text{Cost per set up} = \frac{\$150{,}000}{23{,}000} = \$6.52$$

$$\text{Budgeted unit cost of R:} = \frac{\$6.52 \times 4}{50} = \mathbf{\$0.52}$$

29 The total cost attributed to product Y for component deliveries using the proposed activity based costing system is $2,160

Cost driver	Number of cost drivers	Charge out rate
Number of component deliveries	500 + 600 + 800 = 1,900	$6,840/1,900 = $3.60 per delivery

Charge to Product Y = 600 × $3.6 = $2,160

30 The total cost attributed to product C for quality inspections using an activity based costing system is $8,484

Cost driver	Number of cost drivers	Charge out rate
Number of quality inspections	(200 × 10) + (300 × 20) + (400 × 30) = 20,000	$14,140/20,000 = $0.707 per inspection

Charge to Product C = 400 × 30 × $0.707 = $8,484

31 Advantages of an activity based costing system

Cost	Advantage?
Better cost control is possible	✓
Arbitrary allocations of costs are avoided	
Better product pricing is possible	✓
The choice of cost drivers is easy	
Can be applied to service companies	✓

ABC provides better information on costs and how they are driven. It should therefore facilitate better cost control it can be difficult to attach cost drivers to activities and this can make the system expensive to set up initially. It will also still involve some arbitrary cost allocations. For example, in a service industry it may be difficult to determine what drives the chief executive's salary and to determine how this should be allocated to services.

Despite these faults, ABC should still provide a better allocation of costs to products when compared to traditional costing methods and this should then result in better pricing decisions. The success of ABC in manufacturing industries has led to the adoption of the technique in service industries – and exam questions are just as likely to involve service industries as they are to involve a manufacturing company.

32 B

The cost of the reviewing activity is affected by the number of times the particular activity is undertaken. This is an example of a transaction driver.

33 The cost per unit attributed to product L for processing time is $0.16

Budgeted processing minutes:

Product L (300,000 × 4)	=	1,200,000
Product M (300,000 × 6)	=	1,800,000
Product N (150,000 × 6)	=	900,000
		3,900,000 minutes

Cost per minute= $\frac{\$156{,}000}{3{,}900{,}000}$ =\$0.04

Budgeted unit cost of L = \$0.04 × 4 = **\$0.16**

OTHER ELEMENTS OF COSTING

34 C

$$\text{Return per minute} = \frac{\text{Selling price} - \text{material cost}}{\text{Time on bottleneck resource}} = \frac{50 - 16}{8} = \$4.25$$

Return per hour = $4.25 × 60 = $255

35 The throughput accounting ratio for this product is 0.778.

$$\text{Return per factory hour} = \frac{\$12 - \$5}{0.75 \text{ hours}} = \$9.3333$$

Cost per factory hour = $144,000/12,000 = $12

TA ratio = 9.3333/12 = 0.778

36 A

This is CIMA's Official Terminology definition of a bottleneck. With a throughput accounting approach, the aim should be to reduce or remove bottlenecks, so as to increase throughput.

37 Process **Y** is the bottleneck process.

	Product S	**Product T**
Throughput of process X per day:		
	13.5 hrs × (60/5) = 162.00	13.5 hrs × (60/7.5) = 108.00
(Production time = 15 – 1.5 = 13.5 hours)		
Throughput of process Y per day:		
	14 hrs × (60/18) = 46.67	14 hrs × (60/12) = 70.00
(Production time = 15 – 1 = 14 hours)		

Process Y is the bottleneck process because it limits the production of both products to figures that are less than sales demand.

38 The value of inventory of X at 31 August using a throughput accounting approach is $5,000.

Under throughput accounting, finished goods will be valued at direct material cost.

$$\text{Cost per unit} = \frac{\$40{,}000}{2{,}000 \text{ units}} = \$20 \text{ per unit}$$

No. of units in closing inventory = 2,000 – 1,750 = 250 units.

Therefore, value of closing inventory = 250 units × $20 = $5,000

39 The profit for the period using throughput accounting is $2,750.

Value of closing inventory = $13,500 × 200/2,000 = $1,350

	$	$
Sales		81,000
Material costs	13,500	
Less closing inventory	1,350	
Cost of sales		12,150
Throughput		68,850
Operating expenses		66,100
Net profit		2,750

40 D

Using throughput accounting inventory is valued at material cost

Inventory value = 20,000/4,000 × 400 units = $2,000

41 C

Installing new filters and treatment processes to reduce the toxicity of waste is an example of proactive measures taken to prevent environmental harm.

42 A

Digital products typically have a low or nil marginal cost. They do not typically have high marginal costs.

The other statements are true.

43

	Higher	**Lower**
The life span of the product	✓	
The total indirect labour costs	✓	
Inventory costs		✓
Infrastructure costs	✓	

Digital products typically have longer/higher life spans than physical products as they can be more easily updated with new features. Total indirect labour costs also tend to be higher because of this need to provide ongoing updates and support. There will also be infrastructure costs such as payments to have the product on a particular mobile platform (such costs are typically absent for physical products). But no inventory will be held of digital products and therefore these costs will not exist.

44 A

Digital products typically have a low or nil marginal cost. Marginal costing would not be useful for digital products.

45 B

Although it may happen, it is not common for systems to be linked to those of customers. This would not impact on the costing of the product.

46

	True	**False**
There is a focus on a smaller number of suppliers		✓
Fewer overhead drivers are used		✓
Large volumes of data are processed	✓	
The digital cost can be created very quickly	✓	

Digital costing provides access to a greater number of suppliers. It also provides more details on overheads and has more overhead drivers. But it can deal with large volumes of data and provide products costs almost instantaneously.

VARIANCE ANALYSIS

47 The favourable material price variance is $836.

The standard price per kg = $5

The actual price paid per kg = $82,764 / 16,720 kg = $4.95 per kg

AQAP						
	16,720 kg	×	$4.95/kg	=	$82,764	Price
AQSP						$836 F
	16,720 kg	×	$5 /kg	=	$83,600	

Alternatively:

	$	
16,720 kg did cost	82,764	
16,720 kgs should cost ($5/kg)	83,600	
Price variance	$836	(F)

48 C

Option A is an ideal standard, option B is an attainable standard and option D is a current standard.

49 D

Direct labour variance

AHAR					
	24,000 hrs	×	\$14/hr	=	\$336,000
					Rate
AHSR					\$24,000 F
	24,000 hrs	×	\$15/hr	=	\$360,000

Alternatively:

	\$	
Actual hours paid (24,000) did cost	336,000	
Actual hours paid should cost (\$15/hr)	360,000	
Rate variance	\$24,000	(F)

50 A

Variable overhead efficiency variance

AHSR					
	24,000 hrs	×	\$6/hr	=	\$144,000
					Efficiency
SHSR					\$12,000 A
	2 hrs/unit × 11,000 units	×	\$6/hr	=	\$132,000

51 D

	\$
Budget overhead	2,500,000
Actual overhead	2,010,000
Expenditure variance	490,000 F

52 C

OAR = $2,500,000/500,000 = $5 per unit

Budgeted volume	500,000 units
Actual volume	440,000 units
	60,000 units
× FOAR per unit	× $5
Volume variance	$300,000 A

53 A

	$
Expected cost = (\$800 + (\$0.0002 × $4,100^2$)) × 1.03	4,287
Actual cost	5,000
	713A

54 B

Inventories are valued at standard prices, so the material price variance must be calculated by reference to the quantity purchased. For a usage variance the quantity must be the quantity used (13,050 kgs).

Material variances

AQpAP	12,550 kg			=	$72,900.00	
AQpSP	12,550 kg	×	$6.75/kg	=	$84,712.50	Price $11,812.50 F
AQuSP	13,050 kg		$6.75/kg	=	$88,087.50	
SQSP	6 kg/unit × 2,192 units	×	$6.75/kg	=	$88,776.00	Usage $688.50 F

For a price variance the quantity must be the quantity purchased (13,050 kgs – reduction in inventory = 13,050 – 500 = 12,550 kgs).

Alternatively:

	$	
12,550 kgs should cost ($6.75/kg)	84,712.50	
They did cost	72,900.00	
Price variance	$11,812.50	(F)

	kgs	
Usage variance		
2,192 finished units should use (× 6kg)	13,152	
They did use	13,050	
Usage variance in kgs	102 kgs	(F)

Usage variance in $ = 102 kgs (F) × $6.75/kg (standard price) = $688.50 (F)

55 C

Actual hours paid = 9,760

Actual hours work = 9,480

Difference = 280 hours

Standard rate = $24

Idle time variance = $6,720

56 C

Labour variances

SHSR						
	10 hrs/unit × 6,200 units	×	$9.50/hr	=	$589,000	
						Efficiency
AHSR						$8,455 A
	62,890 hrs	×	$9.50/hr	=	$597,455	
AHAR						Rate
	62,890 hrs			=	$596,412	$1,043 F

The variances could also be calculated as follows:

Rate variance:	$	
62,890 hours should cost (× $9.50)	597,455	
They did cost	596,412	
Labour rate variance	1,043	(F)

Efficiency variance:	**Hours**	
6,200 units should take (× 10)	62,000	
They did take	62,890	
Efficiency variance in hours	890	(A)

Efficiency variance in $ = 890 hours (A) × $9.50 per hour = $8,455 Adverse.

57 The adverse fixed overhead volume variance is $10,000.

Absorption rate= $\frac{\$170,000}{42,500}$ =$4/unit

	Units	
Budgeted output	42,500	
Actual output	40,000	
Volume variance in units	2,500	(A)
Standard fixed overhead cost/unit	× $4	
Fixed overhead volume variance in $	$10,000	(A)

58 The favourable fixed overhead efficiency variance is $24,000.

		Hours	
Standard hours for actual production	(104,040/20,400) × 20,000	102,000	
Less Actual hours		100,000	
Volume variance in units		2,000	(F)
Standard fixed overhead cost/hour	($1,248,480/104,040)	× $12	
Fixed overhead efficiency variance in $		$24,000	(F)

59 B

Actual hours		660	
Less Budgeted hours	2 × 320 ops	640	
Capacity variance in hours		20	(F)
Standard fixed overhead cost/hour	($108,000/[320 × 2 hours])	× $168.75	
Fixed overhead capacity variance in $		$3,375	(F)

60 D

Standard hours for actual production	2 hours × 300 ops	600	
Less Actual hours		660	
Efficiency variance in hours		60	(A)
Standard fixed overhead cost/hour	($108,000/[320 × 2 hours])	× $168.75	
Fixed overhead efficiency variance in $		$10,125	(A)

61 C

Variable overhead expenditure variance

AHSR

8,000 hrs	×	$15/hr	=	$120,000	Expenditure $12,000 A

AHAR

8,000 hrs			=	$132,000	

The variance could also be calculated as follows:

	$	
8,000 hours should cost (× $15)	120,000	
did cost	132,000	
Expenditure variance	12,000	Adverse

62 B

SHSR

0.75 hrs/unit × 11,000 units	×	$20/hr	=	$165,000	Efficiency $5,000 F

AHSR

8,000 hrs	×	$20/hr	=	$160,000	

The variances could be calculated as follows:

	Hours	
11,000 units should take (× 0.75 hr)	8,250	
did take	8,000	
Labour efficiency variance in hours	250	Favourable
Standard rate per hour	× $20	
Labour efficiency variance in $	$5,000	Favourable

63 D

Sales price variance

	$	
Actual units did sell for (642 × $465)	298,530	
Actual units should sell for ($500)	321,000	
Sales price variance	22,470	(A)

64 C

Sales volume contribution variance

	Units	
Actual quantity sold	642	
Budget quantity sold	600	
Sales volume variance in units	42	(F)
× Std contribution per unit (25% × $500)	× $125	
	$5,250	(F)

65 A

The fixed overhead volume variance is the difference between budgeted and actual production volume multiplied by the standard absorption rate per unit. This is the same as the difference between budgeted value of fixed overheads (budgeted volume × standard absorption rate per unit) and standard fixed overheads absorbed by actual production (actual volume × standard absorption rate per unit).

66

		Correct?
(i)	The standard allowance for material wastage was set too high.	
(ii)	Material purchased was of a lower quality than standard.	✓
(iii)	Lower grade and less experienced employees were used than standard.	✓
(iv)	More material was purchased than budgeted for the period because output was higher than budgeted.	

Event (i) is more likely to result in a favourable usage variance therefore it is not correct. Event (ii) could cause an adverse usage variance since a lower quality material might lead to higher wastage and a higher level of quality control rejects. Event (iii) could cause an adverse usage variance because lower skilled employees might waste material and quality control rejects might again be higher. Event (iv) would not necessarily cause an adverse usage variance. The usage variance is based on the expected usage for the actual output, not on the budgeted usage for the budgeted output.

67 The favourable inspection efficiency variance for December is $4,000.

Total budgeted inspections = $30,000 / $200 = 150 inspections

Standard inspections on actual output = 150 × 1,200 units / 1,000 units = 180 inspections

Efficiency variance = (180 inspections – 160 inspections) × $200 per inspection = $4,000 favourable

68 B

Less experienced employees are likely to take longer than standard to produce a given level of output. The result would be an adverse variable overhead efficiency variance. Option A is more likely to result in a favourable variable overhead efficiency variance because employees are likely to work faster than standard. Option C might also result in a favourable efficiency variance because higher quality material is likely to be easier to process, thus saving time against standard. Option D would result in an adverse variable overhead expenditure variance but would not directly affect the variable overhead efficiency variance.

69 The favourable sales volume profit variance for the period was $20,000.

Sales volume profit variance

Budgeted sales volume (units)	100,000	
Actual sales volume (units)	110,000	
	10,000	F
Standard profit per unit ($10 – $8)	$2	
	$20,000	F

70 D

The question is telling us two things: firstly, that actual hours were greater than budgeted hours, and, secondly, that actual hours were more than the standard hours. The first point would lead to a favourable fixed overhead capacity variance. The second point would result in an adverse labour efficiency and fixed overhead efficiency variances. If the standard hours are 100 more than the original budget, then it would result in a favourable fixed overhead volume variance.

71 The idle time variance for April was $49,500.

Idle hours = 61,500 – 56,000 = 5,500

Standard rate per hour = $540,000/60,000 = $9

Idle time variance = 5,500 × $9 = $49,500 Adverse

72

Variance
Material price variance
Material usage variance
Labour rate variance
Labour efficiency variance

Cause
Increase in costs charged by a supplier
Increased wastage due to a machine malfunction
Unexpected pay award
Improved operating procedures for staff

An increase in costs from a supplier would cause an adverse material price variance. Increased wastage would cause an adverse material usage variance but might not affect labour efficiency. An unexpected pay award would give an adverse labour rate variance, and improved operating procedures would make the staff more efficient and as such a favourable efficiency variance.

73

	Caused by purchasing better quality?
Favourable fixed overhead expenditure variance	
Favourable material usage variance	✓
Adverse labour rate variance	
Favourable labour efficiency variance	✓
Favourable labour rate variance	

74 B

It is usual for the purchasing department to negotiate prices with suppliers. So if a supplier is charging more than the standard price this would fall under the responsibility of the purchasing manager.

Better quality materials should result in less wastage of material which in turn will allow the employees to produce more units in the time allowed as fewer units will be scrapped or require rework.

75 A

It is usual for the production manager to finalise the production schedule so if the labour has been less efficient than expected then this would be his/her/their responsibility.

76

	Affected?
Sales price variance	
Sales quantity profit variance	✓
Fixed overhead expenditure variance	
Fixed overhead capacity variance	✓

The difference in between marginal and absorption costing is in the treatment of fixed overheads. This will impact on the profit per unit which will impact on the sales quantity profit variance. In marginal costing there is no fixed overhead volume variance and therefore there would be no fixed overhead capacity variance.

77 The expenditure variance for the set ups was $100.

Standard price (SP) = 6,820/220 = 31

Flexed standard cost = AQ × SP = 200 × $31 = 6,200

Actual cost = 6,300

Variance = 6,200 – 6,300 = $100A

78 The favourable variable overhead efficiency variance is $3,000

Number of hours per unit for Product X = $14/$7 = 2 hours

Number of hours per unit for Product Y = $10.50/$7 = 1.5 hours

Variable overhead cost per hour = $3/2 hours (or $2.25/1.5 hours) = $1.50 per hour

Variable overhead efficiency variance =

((12,000 × 2 hrs) + (16,000 × 1.5 hrs)) – 46,000) × $1.50 per hour = $3,000 Favourable

79 B

Standard quantity (SQ) = 75 supervisors/5,000 employees × 5,500 employees = 82.5 supervisors

Standard price (SP) = $7,500/75 supervisors = $100 per supervisor

Standard cost (SQ × SP) = 82.5 × $100 = $8,250

Actual cost = $8,085

Total variance = 8,250 – 8,085 = $165 Favourable

80 The favourable sales price variance is $17,400

Sales price variance

	$	
Actual output did sell for	365,400	
Actual output should sell for (58 × $6,000)	348,000	
Sales price variance	17,400	(F)

81 B

When using a marginal costing system, the sales volume variance will be based on the standard contribution per unit.

The volume variance is 5,000 units, and the total value = 5,000 × 20 = $100,000

82 The total adverse materials variance was $32,200

Expected materials cost per poster = 6 × $10 = $60

Total expected cost for the actual campaign = $60 × 20,000 posters = $1,200,000

Actual cost = $1,232,200

Total variance = 1,200,000 – 1,232,200 = $32,200 adverse

83 The adverse labour rate variance is $3,900

	$	
Actual hours (1,950) did cost	120,900	
Actual hours should cost (1,950 × $60)	117,000	
Labour rate variance	3,900	(A)

84 D

The standard cost for the 240,000 actual units produced = 240,000 × $10 = $2.4m

The actual cost = $2.51m

Total variance = $2.4m – $2.51m = $110,000 adverse

85 B

If the actual profit for the month was $120,000, to calculate the budgeted profit we need to work backwards and deduct favourable variances and add adverse variances.

	$
Actual profits	120,000
Sales volume variance	(7,000)
Materials price variance	(2,500)
Labour efficiency variance	4,000
Fixed overhead expenditure variance	1,700
Budgeted profit for June	**116,200**

FURTHER VARIANCE ANALYSIS

86 The actual rate paid per direct labour hour for the period was $12.75

11,500 units should use 5 hours each	57,500 hours
Did use	?
Variance in hours	
Value at $12 per hour	
Labour efficiency variance	$30,000 A

Working backwards:

The variance in hours = $30,000/$12 = 2,500 A

The actual hours used are 57,500 + 2,500 = 60,000

60,000 hours should cost (× $12)	720,000
Did cost	?
Labour rate variance	45,000 A

Working backwards:

The actual labour cost = $765,000

So the actual rate paid per hour = $765,000/60,000 = $12.75.

87 The total favourable sales mix profit variance for the period is $50.

Product	Actual sales actual mix	Actual sales standard mix	Variance (units)	Standard profit/unit	Sales mix variance
A	750	725	25 (F)	$5.00	$125.00 (F)
B	700	725	25 (A)	$3.00	$75.00 (A)
Total	1,450	1,450			$50.00 (F)

Where the standard mix is the total actual sales units (1,450) divided by the total budgeted sales units (1,600) and multiplied by the budgeted units of each individual product (800 for A)

88 The total favourable sales quantity profit variance for the period is $5,130.

Standard weighted average profit per unit:

Product	Sales budget (units)	Standard profit/unit	Total profit
A	3,000	$2.00	$6,000
B	8,000	$1.50	$12,000
C	9,000	$1.80	$16,200
Total	20,000		$34,200

Average profit per unit = $34,200/20,000 units = $1.71 per unit

Sales quantity profit variance

Budgeted sales units	20,000	
Actual sales units	23,000	
	3,000	(F)
Average profit per unit	$1.71	
Sales quantity profit variance	$5,130	(F)

89 The favourable sales mix profit variance for Product B is $26,250.

	Actual sales @standard mix (units)	Actual sales @ actual mix (units)	Variance (units)	Standard profit $	Variance $
Product B	2,475	3,000	525 F	50.00	**26,250 F**
Product C	2,025	1,500	525 A	53.75	28,219 A
	4,500	4,500			1,969 A

90 D

Total budgeted profit = ($4 × 4,000) + ($3 × 6,000) = $34,000

Weighted average profit per unit = $34,000/10,000 = $3.40

Sales quantity profit variance

Budgeted sales units	10,000	
Actual sales units	12,000	
	2,000	(F)
Average profit per unit	$3.40	
Sales quantity profit variance	$6,800	(F)

91 The adverse material price planning variance was $4,480.

Material price planning variance

Revised budget 1,600 units × 7kg per unit × $4.50	$50,400
Original budget 1,600 units × 7kg per unit × $4.10	$45,920
	$4,480 A

92 C

SQSP	6kg/unit × 600 units	×	$3/kg	=	$10,800	
						Usage $450 F
AQSP	?	×	$3/kg	=	?	
						Price $2,000 F
AQAP	?			=	?	

This is a 'backwards' question. Given some information including the variances, we then have to work backwards to find some missing numbers – here, the number of kg purchased.

SQSP	6kg/unit × 600 units	×	$3/kg	=	$10,800	
						Usage $450 F
AQSP	3,450 kg (Bal 2)	×	$3/kg	=	10,350 (Bal 1)	
						Price $2,000 F
AQAP				=		

The question can also be answered as follows:

	Kg	
600 units should use (× 6 kg)	3,600	
Usage variance in kg ($450(F)/3)	150	(F)
Therefore 600 units did use	3,450	

Given no change in stock levels, usage quantity = purchase quantity.

93 B

As this is an operational variance, the standards used are the revised standards.

AQAP	32,000 kg	×	$4.80/kg	=	$153,600	Price $6,400 F
AQSP	32,000 kg	×	$5/kg	=	$160,000	
SQSP	3kg/unit × 10,000 units	×	$5/kg	=	$150,000	Usage $10,000 A

94 B

	Planning		Operational	
Original		Revised Standard		Actual
$4		$5		$4.80

Planning price variance = ($4 – $5) × 3 kg × 10,000 units = $30,000 A

95 The total adverse sales quantity profit variance for the period using the individual units method is $600.

Product	Sales budget (units)	Standard profit/unit	Total profit
A	800	$5.00	$4,000
B	800	$3.00	$2,400
Total	1,600		$6,400

Weighted average profit per unit = $6,400/1,600 units = $4.00 per unit

Sales quantity profit variance

Budgeted sales units	1,600	
Actual sales units	1,450	
	150	A
Average profit per unit	$4	
Sales quantity profit variance	$600	A

96 D

As this is an operational variance, the standards used are the revised standards.

AQAP							
	32,000 kg	×	$4.80/kg	=	$153,600		Price $6,400 F
AQSP							
	32,000 kg	×	$5/kg	=	$160,000		
SQSP							Usage $10,000 A
	3kg/unit × 10,000 units	×	$5/kg	=	$150,000		

97 The adverse operational material usage variance was $3,600.

Operational material usage variance

1,600 units should use (× 7kg)	11,200 kg	
did use	12,000 kg	
	800 kg A	
Valued at revised standard price ($4.50)		$3,600 A

98 The favourable sales mix variance for concessions for the exhibition is $12,000

Ticket type	**Actual sales @ actual mix**	**Actual sales standard mix**	**Variance (units)**	**Standard cont/unit**	**Sales mix variance**
Full price	12,000	15,000	3,000 (A)	$9.00	$27,000 (A)
Concession	8,000	5,000	3,000 (F)	$4.00	**$12,000 (F)**
Total	20,000	20,000			$15,000 (A)

99 A

As this is an operational variance, the standards used are the revised standards.

SHSR						
	12/60 hrs × 370	×	$10/hr	=	$740	Efficiency $60 A
AHSR						
	80 hrs	×	$10/hr	=	$800	

100 C

By selling less electric-powered cars, there has been a change in the sales mix in which a lower proportion of sales have come from the electric-powered cars and a higher proportion came from the diesel-powered car. The diesel-powered car has a higher contribution per car ($5,000) than the electric-powered car ($4,000). This would give a favourable sales mix contribution variance. However, there would be an adverse sales quantity contribution variance because less cars have been sold in total.

101 The actual level of production for the period was 360,000 units

	$
Actual overhead	1,950,000
Overhead absorbed	?
Actual output × $5	
Under absorbed	150,000

OAR = $1,500,000/300,000 = $5 per unit

Fixed production overhead variance is the level of over/under absorption. An adverse variance means that overhead is under absorbed. If actual overheads were $1,950,000 and were under-absorbed by $150,000, then only $1,800,000 must have been absorbed.

Overheads absorbed = units produced × FOAR per unit

$1,800,000 = units produced × $5

Units produced = $1,800,000 / $5 = 360,000 units.

102 The actual quantity of materials purchased in May was 8,630 kg

Materials price variance pro-forma:

	$
Actual quantity purchased did cost	56,000
Actual quantity purchased should cost	?
(actual quantity × $6)	
Materials price variance	4,220 A

An adverse price variance means that materials cost more than standard. They should therefore have only cost $56,000 – $4,220 = $51,780.

If the standard cost per kg is $6 then the actual quantity purchased must have been $51,780/ $6 = 8,630 kg.

103 B, E

The original standard time per set of accounts was 10 hours.

The revised standard time per set of accounts was 10 × 0.75 = 7.5 hours.

Statement A is incorrect. The planning variance is the difference between the original standard time for actual output (200 sets of accounts @ 10 hours each = 2,000 hours) and the revised standard time for actual output (200 sets of accounts @ 7.5 hours each = 1,500 hours), charged at the standard cost of each labour hour. As the revised standard time is less than the original standard time, this results in a favourable planning variance.

Statement B is correct. The operational labour efficiency variance is the difference between the actual time taken to produce actual output (1,400 hours) and the revised standard time for actual output (200 sets × 7.5 hours = 1,500 hours), charged at the standard cost of each hour. As the actual time taken was less than the revised standard, this results in a favourable variance.

Statement C is incorrect. We do not have information in the question about the labour rates and so are not able to determine whether the operational labour rate variances are favourable or adverse.

Statement D is incorrect.

Statement E is correct, as per the description above in relation to statement B.

BUDGETING AND BUDGETARY CONTROL

PREPARING BUDGETS

104

	Purpose of budgeting?
Communication	✓
Authorisation	✓
Sales maximisation	
Co-ordination	✓

The budget communicates to individual managers what is expected of them in the forthcoming budget period and how much expenditure they can incur in meeting their targets. Thus communication is a purpose of budgeting. An agreed budget provides authorisation for individual managers to incur expenditure in undertaking the activities in their own budget centre. Therefore, authorisation is a purpose of budgeting. Although an organisation might have an objective of maximising sales and might set a budget to enable them to achieve this objective, the maximisation of sales is not in itself a purpose of budgeting. Therefore, this is not correct. Individual budget targets are set within the framework of the plan for the organisation as a whole and in this way a budget provides a means of coordinating the efforts of everyone within the organisation.

105 B

The cash budget is part of the master budget.

The other statements are all true.

106 D

Sales units:

	1	**2**	**3**
Sales units	2,500	3,000	4,000

Opening inventory = 10% of quarter 2 sales = 10% × 3,000 = 300

Closing inventory = 10% of quarter 3 sales = 10% × 4,000 = 400

Production = sales + closing inventory – opening inventory

= 3,000 + 400 – 300 = 3,100 units

107 C

Note that the material usage figure is not required.

	Units
Sales	30,000
Add closing inventory (3,500 × 1.35)	4,725
Less opening inventory	(3,500)
Production	31,225

108 A

The increasing use of electronic devices makes big data collection easier. Many organisations successfully gather information from social media sites such as Facebook and Twitter and use it to great effect within their decision-making processes.

109

	E	**F**	**G**	**Total**
Budgeted number of batches to be produced:	75,000/200 = 375	120,000/60 = 2,000	60,000/30 = 2,000	
Machine set-ups per batch:	5	3	9	
Total machine set-ups	1,875	6,000	18,000	25,875

So budgeted cost per set-up: $180,000/25,875 = $6.96 per set-up

Therefore, the budgeted machine set-up cost per unit of F produced is:

($6.96 × 3)/60 = $0.35 per unit or $6.96 × 6,000/120,000 = $0.35 per unit

110 D

111 The expected level of production in May is 15,900 units

	April	May	June
Production budget (units)			
Sales	12,000	15,000	18,000
Add closing inventory	4,500	5,400	
	16,500	20,400	
Less opening inventory	3,600	4,500	
Production	12,900	15,900	

112 A

Beyond budgeting makes greater use of rolling budgets to create an environment of continuous planning. It also has more local budget setting (rather than a top-down approach), uses a greater number of targets (rather than simply focusing on financial targets) and seeks continuous improvements (rather than standardisation).

113 B

A zero based budgeting system begins each budget from scratch every time. All expenditure on the activity must be justified from zero and the method of carrying out each activity must be re-evaluated as if it were being carried out for the first time.

114 C

Probability of rainy summer = $1.0 - 0.4 = 0.6$

Expected value of sales volume = $(80,000 \times 0.4) + (120,000 \times 0.6)$

= 104,000 units

115

	True	False
Big data management involves using sophisticated systems to gather, store and analyse large volumes of data	✓	
Data can be in variety of structured and unstructured formats.	✓	
Big data does not include traditional data from internal sources such as sales history, preferences, order frequency and pricing information.		✓
Big data does include information from external sources such as websites, trade publications and social networks.	✓	

116 D

Only cash receipts and cash payments should be included in the cash budget. When fixtures and fittings are sold the proceeds from the sale of the fixtures and fittings represent the cash received from the sale. The profit from the sale is the difference between the proceeds and the carrying value of the asset.

117 The budgeted cost per month for quality testing is $34,000

$$\text{The monthly variance} = \frac{\$102{,}000}{12 \text{ months}} = \$8{,}500$$

$$\text{The variance number of tests} = \frac{\$8{,}500}{\$850 \text{ per test}} = 10 \text{ tests}$$

Budgeted tests must therefore have been = 50 – 10 = 40 per month.

Budgeted quality test costs per month = 40 tests × $850 per test = $34,000

118 D

This is the definition of a master budget.

119 The entry for 'purchases' that will be shown in the cash budget for August is $76,000

Purchases are sold at cost plus 25% so cost of sales is 100/125= 0.8 × sales

Closing inventory = 0.5 × following month's cost of sales

Closing inventory = Opening inventory of the following month

Month	**Sales**	**Cost of sales**	**Opening inventory**	**Closing inventory**	**Purchase**	**Paid**
July	100	80	40	36	76	
August	90	72	36	50	86	**76**

120 The total receipts expected in month 3 are $114,144

	Sales	$
Cash receipts	$108,000 × 20%	21,600
Month 2	$120,000 × 80% × 40% × 0.985	37,824
Month 1	$105,000 × 80% × 58% (see note)	48,720
B/f		6,000
		$114,144

Note: 98% of credit sales are received within 2 months. This will include the 40% of credit sales which were received within 1 month, with the remaining 58% of credit sales being received in the second month.

121 The total budgeted delivery cost for the next period is $1,694,000

This year's cost per delivery was = $1,400,000 / 5,000 deliveries = $280 per delivery

Next year's cost per delivery is $280 × 1.10 = $308

Next year's total delivery costs will be $308 per delivery × 5,500 deliveries = $1,694,000

122 A

Inspection costs are a semi-variable cost which will have both fixed and variable elements.

Although there will be some reduction in the total cost, the fixed element of this cost will stay the same and this fixed cost will need to be shared out between a smaller number of inspections overall. This will increase the average cost per inspection and subsequently increase the inspection costs allocated to Product A and Product B.

Meanwhile, Product C should still benefit from a reduction in inspection costs because of the reduced number of inspections. However, the decision is likely to lead to an increase in customer returns for Product C if any quality defects are not identified before the product is sold as a result of the reduced number of inspections.

123 The labour cost budget for the year is $2,112,000

Labour hours for production

36,000 units × 4 hours = 144,000 hours

Idle time = 10% of total available hours, therefore total available hours need to be:

144,000 hours/0.9 = 160,000 hours

Labour cost budget ($)

160,000 hours × 20% = 32,000 hours × ($12 × 1.50) = $576,000

160,000 hours × 80% = 128,000 hours × $12 = $1,536,000

The total labour cost budget = 576,000 + 1,536,000 = $2,112,000

124 The direct labour cost budget for the next year is $40,000

Budgeted production of Product Y	1,800	units
Hours per unit	2	hours
Total production time required	3,600	hours
Adjust for idle time	×100/90	
Total direct labour time	4,000	hours
Rate per hour	$10	
Total direct labour cost	$40,000	

125 C

	$
Cash received from previous period	460,000
Sales for this budget period	5,400,000
	5,860,000
Credit sales not paid until next period ($5,400,000 × 80% × 1/12)	(360,000)
Total cash received	5,500,000

126 The revised contribution from Gold packages is $300,000

Sales revenue and variable costs per unit (original budget):

	Silver	**Gold**
	$ per package	$ per package
Sales revenue	1,000	2,000
Variable cost	400	1,000
Contribution	600	1,000

Revised sales mix:

Silver packages = 25% × $800,000 = $200,000 = 200 packages

Gold packages = 75% × $800,000 = $600,000 = 300 packages

Revised contribution from Gold packages = 300 × $1,000 = $300,000

127 The answer is $

Fee income	$150,000
Staff costs ($65,625 × 1.04)	($68,250)
Other direct costs	($28,125)
Overhead costs	($42,188)
Revised gross profit	$11,437

Change in gross profit = $14,062 – $11,437 = $2,625

Change as a percentage of original budget = $2,625 / $14,062 × 100 = 18.67%

128 B

129

Cost
Commission paid to an agent for selling the product
Electricity used in the factory
Depreciation of factory building
Packaging material to protect the product

Budget
Selling overhead budget
Variable production overhead budget
Fixed production overhead budget
Distribution overhead budget

130 The entry for 'purchases' that will be shown in the cash budget for September is $86,000

Purchases are sold at cost plus 25% so cost of sales is 100/125= 0.8 × Sales

Opening inventory = 0.5 × this month's cost of sales

Closing inventory = 0.5 × following month's cost of sales

Closing inventory = Opening inventory of the following month

Month	**Sales**	**Cost of sales**	**Opening inventory**	**Closing inventory**	**Purchase**	**Paid**
August	90	72	36	50	86	
September	125	100	50	56	106	**86**

131 C

	$
Cash paid from previous period	540,000
Purchases for this budget period	6,800,000
	7,340,000
Purchases not paid until next period ($6,800,000 × 75% × 1/12)	(425,000)
Total cash paid	6,915,000

132 A

The annual rent for the head office building is an administrative overhead not a production overhead, the electricity usage would be a variable production overhead rather than a fixed production overhead, and the materials is a direct cost rather than an overhead.

133 C

The direct material and the royalty fee are both direct costs and therefore not included with in the overhead budget.

134 The budgeted fixed overheads in the period were $200,000

As the overheads are absorbed on a labour hours' basis, the number of units and machine hours are irrelevant. So the budget will be 16,000 hours × $12.50 per hour = $200,000

135 C

Total labour hours = (1,000 units × 0.5 hours) + (2,000 units × 2 hours) = 4,500 hours

Total machine hours = (1,000 units × 0.25 hours) + 2,000 units × 1.5 hours) = 3,250 hours

Total variable overheads = 3,250 hours × $1.50 per hour = $4,875

Total fixed overheads = 4,500 hours × $1.95 per hour = $8,775

Total overheads = $4,875 + $8,775 = $13,650

136

	Not a criticism?
It may make managers, staff and unions feel threatened	✓
It encourages slack	
It is time consuming as it involves starting from scratch	✓
It encourages wasteful spending	
It includes past inefficiencies as costs are not scrutinised	

ZBB may make staff feel threatened as they need to justify all costs and activities. This is less likely with incremental budgeting. Incremental budgeting is not a slow process, as budgets are based on prior period figures.

137

	Characteristic of rolling budgets?
Budgets are more likely to be realistic as there is a shorter period between preparation and actual events occurring	
Updates to budgets are only made when they are foreseeable	✓
They reduce uncertainty in budgeting	
They force management to look ahead more frequently	
Each item of expenditure must be fully justified before inclusion in the budget	✓

Rolling budgets are updated on as regular basis (for example, monthly or quarterly), not just when a change is foreseeable. The final point is a characteristic of zero based budgeting.

138 D

Zero based budgeting is the method in which all activities are re-evaluated.

139 D

140 D

Month	**1**	**2**	**3**
Production units	1,850	1,800	2,020
Rate per unit	$1.20	$1.20	$1.20
Variable overhead cost	$2,220	$2,160	$2,424
60% in month	1,332	1,296	1,454
40% in following month		888	864
Payment	1,332	2,184	2,318

141 The sales receipts for month 2 are budgeted to be $10,180

Month	**1**	**2**	**3**
Sales units	1,500	1,750	2,000
Sales (Units × $10)	15,000	17,500	20,000
Paid in month – 20% × 0.98	2,940	3,430	3,920
45% in the following month		6,750	7,875
25% in 3rd month			3,750
Receipts	2,940	10,180	15,545

142 C

	Original	**Adjustment**	**Revised**
	$000		$000
Revenue	720	Less: $720 × 30% = $216	504
Cost of sales	324	Less: $216 × 100/120 = $180	144
Other operating costs	120		120
Net profit	276		240

FORECASTING

143 D

	Units	**Total cost**
High	800	$4,700
Low	500	$3,500
	300	$1,200

Total variable cost = difference in cost / difference in activity = $1,200/300 = $4.00.

Total fixed cost = $4,700 – (800 × $4.00) = $1,500

144 D

Year 7, quarter 3 is period 27

Trend sales = 25,000 + 6,500 × 27
= 200,500 units

Adjusted for seasonal variations = 200,500 × 150% = 300,750 units

145 D

If no money is spent on advertising, then sales revenue would be $150,000.

$7,000 is the additional revenue that will be generated for every $1 increase in advertising spend (x). This is the variable element in the equation. $150,000 is the fixed element; even if activity (x) is zero, the value of y (sales) will still be $150,000.

146 C

Total production overhead costs (20X5 prices) = $127,000 + ($18.6 × 4,600 hours) = $212,560

As the regression equation is based on 20X5 prices, then we need to restate at 20X6 prices

Total production overhead costs (20X6 prices) = $212,560 × (225/205) = $233,298

147 B

Firstly, strip out the 5% wage increase included in the Month 2 cost.

Month 2 uninflated wage cost = $2,982,000 / 1.05 = $2,840,000

Now apply the usual high-low technique

Variable cost per hour = ($2,840,000 – $2,420,000)/(190,000 – 160,000)
= $420,000/30,000
= $14 per hour

Inflated for 5% wage rise = $14 × 1.05 = $14.70 per hour

Alternatively, Month 1's total cost could be inflated by 5% instead.

Month 1 inflated wage cost = $2,420,000 × 1.05 = $2,541,000

Now apply the usual high-low technique

Variable cost per hour = ($2,982,000 – $2,541,000)/(190,000 – 160,000)
= $441,000/30,000
= $14.70 per hour

148 The overhead cost for RP for month 240 is $39,000

Orders = [100,000 + (30 × 240)] × 1.08 = 115,776

Overhead cost = $10,000 + ($0.25 × 115,776) = $38,944

149 D

Trend	=	9.72 + (5.816 × 23)
	=	143.488
Seasonal factor	+	6.5
Forecast		149.988

To the nearest whole unit, the forecast number of units to be sold is 150.

150 D

Quarter	**Value of x**		**Trend units**			**Forecast sales units**
4	28	y = (26 × 28) + 8,850	9,578	× 115%	=	11,014.7
1	25	y = (26 × 25) + 8,850	9,500	× 85%	=	8,075.0
						2,939.7

151 B

$$\text{Variable cost per unit} = \frac{\text{Change in cost}}{\text{Change in units}} = \frac{113{,}000 - 55{,}000}{3{,}000 - 1{,}000} = \$29.00 \text{ per unit}$$

Total fixed cost

Total cost @ 3,000 units	113,000
Less variable cost (3,000 units × $29.00/unit)	87,000
Total fixed cost	$26,000

Flexed budget for 2,750 units

Variable cost (2,750 units × $29.00/unit)	79,750
Fixed cost	26,000
Total cost	$105,750

152

89% of the variation in production costs from one month to the next can be explained by corresponding variation in output.	✓
Costs increase as output increases.	
The linear relationship between output and costs is very strong.	✓
An increase of 100% in output is associated with an increase of 89% in costs.	
An increase of 89% in output is associated with an increase of 100% in costs.	

A coefficient of determination between output and production costs, tells us that 89% of the variation in production costs from one month to the next can be explained by corresponding variation in output. It also tells us that the linear relationship between output and costs is very strong. Only a positive correlation can tell us that costs increase as output increases and we cannot assume this from the coefficient of determination.

153 C

Firstly, strip out the inflationary increase included in the Month 2 cost

Production units	1,000	2,000
Budgeted materials cost	$18,000	$24,000 × (100/125) = $19,200
Cost index	100	125

Now apply the usual high-low technique

$$\text{Variable cost per unit} = \frac{\text{Change in cost}}{\text{Change in units}} = \frac{19{,}200 - 18{,}000}{2{,}000 - 1{,}000} = \$1.20 \text{ per unit}$$

Total fixed cost

Total cost @ 2,000 units	19,200
Less variable cost (2,000 units × $1.20/unit)	2,400
Total fixed cost	$16,800

Flexed budget for 2,600 units

Variable cost (2,600 units × $1.2/unit)	3,120
Fixed cost	16,800
Total cost	$19,920

Adjusted for cost index $19,920 × 142/100 = $28,286

154 A, C

Statement B is incorrect. Linear regression only measures the relationship between two variables.

Statement D is incorrect. Only interpolated forecasts tend to be reliable. The equation should not be used for extrapolation.

Statement E is incorrect. Interpolated predictions are only reliable is there is a significant correlation between the data.

155 D

Year 2, quarter 2 is month x = 6

Trend sales = $1,450 + ($55 × 6)
= $1,780

Adjusted for seasonal variations = 1,780 × 115% = $2,047

BUDGETARY CONTROL

156

	Limitations of sensitivity analysis?
Only one variable changes at a time	✓
It assesses the risk to the closing cash balance	
It provides an assessment of how responsive the cash flows are to changes in variables.	
Probabilities of changes are not accounted for	✓
It directs attention to critical variables	

The other options are advantages of using sensitivity analysis.

157 C

Budgetary slack is also called budget bias. Budget holders may sometimes try to obtain a budget that is easier to achieve. They may do this either by bidding for expenditure in excess of what they actually need or, in the case of sales budgets, by deliberately setting easy revenue targets.

158 C

Revised fixed costs = $1,600k – $400k + $250k + $900k (20% × cost of sales) = $2,350k

Contribution = ($6,800k – $3,600) × 60% = $1,920k

Revised profit / (loss) = $1,920k $2,350k = ($430k)

Fall in profit = $700 + $430k = $1,130k

159 The total adverse profit variance for the period was $5,040

	Original budget	Flexed budget	Actual	Variances
Sales units	1,000	1,380	1,380	
Sales revenue	100,000	138,000	133,860	4,140 (A)
Direct material	40,000	55,200	57,800	2,600 (A)
Direct labour	20,000	27,600	27,000	600 (F)
Variable overhead	15,000	20,700	18,600	2,100 (F)
Fixed overhead	10,000	10,000	11,000	1,000 (A)
Profit	15,000	24,500	19,460	5,040 (A)

160 D

A is a fixed budget. B is a zero based budget. C is a flexed budget

161 A

This is an example of feed-forward control, as the manager is using a forecast to assist in making a future decision.

162 B

	Original Budget	Flexed Budget
Sales units	1,000	1,200
	$	$
Sales revenue	100,000	120,000
Direct material	40,000	48,000
Direct labour	20,000	24,000
Variable overhead	15,000	18,000
Fixed overhead	10,000	10,000
Profit	15,000	20,000

163 A

164 B

The other options are all advantages of participative budgeting.

165 C

The other options would all be outcomes of unethical behaviour in budgeting.

166 C

The net cash flow in month 4 will fall by $300k. This will increase the closing cash balance to $410,000. This is $160k above the overdraft limit of $250k.

167 The revised cash receipts in March would be $62,200

Month	**March**
Paid in month – 15% × 0.95	5,700
55% in the following month	38,500
30% in 3rd month	18,000
Receipts	62,200

168 Statement 1 is false, it that would be feedback control. Statement 2 is true, feed-forward control can occur whilst the activity is in progress.

	True	False
Feed-forward control systems have an advantage over other types of control in that it establishes how effective planning was.		✓
Feed-forward control occurs while an activity is in progress.	✓	

169 The new budgeted production in July would be 9,300 units.

Production budget (units)	**July**
Sales	9,000
Add closing inventory	1,200
Less opening inventory	900
Production	9,300

170 A, D

The manager of the purchasing department should only be appraised on those costs that are in his/her/their control. These would include costs such as the cost of raw materials purchased and the cost of employees within the purchasing department. The rental agreements for property/factories are likely to be entered into by head office and not under the control of the purchasing manager. Similarly, any advertising campaigns will be undertaken by head office or sales department and not under the direct control of the purchasing manager.

171 A, D

Statement A is correct. If a manager feels that the targets are too difficult then this may result in the manager giving up before they have started.

Statement B is incorrect. Managers may put their own goals (for example meeting the profit for the period) ahead of the organisations overall objectives.

Statement C is incorrect. For budgetary control to be effective, there should be fairly short reporting periods (for example, monthly). This ensures timely measurement of performance and feedback to managers.

Statement D is correct. If managers are involved in the budget setting process this should increase motivation, commitment and performance.

SHORT TERM COMMERCIAL DECISION MAKING

RELEVANT COSTS AND DECISION MAKING

172 B

The material is in regular use by the organisation and so would be replaced if it is used on the special order. The material is readily available at a price of $3.24 per kg.

Therefore the relevant cost of the material is 1,250 kgs × $3.24 = $4,050.

173 D

Replacement material cost saved (4 kg @ $5.00)	20.00
Less further processing cost ($0.75 × 5 kg)	3.75
Value of M in current use, for each unit made	$16.25

Therefore, opportunity cost of using M on the job is = $16.25/5 kg = $3.25 per kg.

174 The expected relevant cost of Material XY for use when evaluating the viability of the contract is $12,900

If contract is carried out and stock is needed, relevant cost is the replacement value of $15,000. Probability = 0.6

If contract is carried out and stock is not needed, relevant cost is the sales value of $12,000. Probability = 0.4

Whatever happens, $900 holding cost is incurred. This will be saved if the contract is carried out.

Expected value = $15,000 × 0.6 + $12,000 × 0.4 – $900 = $12,900.

175 B

The book value is an historic cost and therefore not relevant. There is no intention to replace material X. There are two options for material X, scrap at a value of 50p per kg or use as a replacement for material Y, which would save $4 per kg ($6 – $2). The latter is the preferable option so the relevant cost is $4 per kg for 10 kgs = $40.

176 C

Labour is in short supply so there is an opportunity cost. The contribution from Contract Z will still be earned but will be delayed. The relevant cost is therefore the wages earned plus the penalty fee.

($15 × 100) + ($1,000) = $2,500

177 A

It is cheaper to hire the external consultant for $4,500 rather than pay the $5,000 bonus to the existing junior consultant. The consultant's salary is not a relevant cost as the consultant will still be paid even if the project does not proceed.

178 The relevant cost of the 2,000 kgs of material J to be included in the quotation is $16,000

Since material J is in regular use and is readily available in the market, its relevant cost is the replacement price of $8/kg.

So 2,000 kgs × $8/kg = $16,000

179 B

Global businesses may have to adopt different ethical approaches in different markets. What is considered good ethical practice in one country may not be considered ethical in another. This may give a lack of global consistency.

The other statements are true.

180 A

3,700 kg × $3.80 + 500 kg × $6.30 = $17,210

Tutorial note

The company needs 4,200 kg. It has 3,700 kg in inventory. It will therefore need to buy 500 kg and these can be bought for $6.30 per kg.

The tricky bit is the value to the company of the 3,700 kg in inventory. The $4.50 original purchase price is of course a sunk cost and cannot be relevant.

The inventory can be sold for $3.20 per kg, so this is its very minimum value. The inventory is worth $3.20 per kg unless the company has an even better alternative.

Well, there is a better alternative. The company can take the inventory and, by spending $3.70 per kg on it, can turn it into something worth $7.50 per kg. If something will be worth $7.50 if we spend $3.70 on it, then it is at present worth $3.80. This then is the value of the inventory to the company and to fulfil the contract the company will use 3,700 kg of inventory with a value of $3.80 per kg.

181 A

This would not impact on cash flows. The other options would increase or decrease cash.

182 D

$\$10.50 + \frac{\$10}{2}$ (W1) = $15.50

(W1) We are told that the labour will have to be diverted from the alternative product. The new product requires $4 of labour. The alternative requires $8 of labour so takes twice as long to produce.

Therefore, to make ONE new product we need to stop making HALF an alternative product. Therefore, the relevant cost of labour for ONE item of new product is HALF the lost contribution of the alternative.

Relevant cost of labour = $10/2 = $5

183 The cost per unit of product Y is $74

By-product revenue = 3,000 × $0.20 = $600.

Therefore, costs of the process = $45,000 – $600 = $44,400.

		$
Sales revenue, product X	= 250 × $80 =	20,000
Sales revenue, product Y	= 400 × $100 =	40,000
Total joint product sales revenue =		60,000

Joint costs are apportioned:

To X: $44,400 × 20/60 = $14,800

To Y: $44,400 × 40/60 = $29,600.

Cost per unit of product Y = $29,600/400 = $74.

184 D

	$/unit
Direct materials	9.00
Direct labour	14.00
Total direct cost	23.00
Production overhead absorbed (2 hours × $4.50 per hour)	9.00
Total production cost	32.00
Mark-up for non-production costs (10% × $32)	3.20
Full cost	35.20
Profit mark-up (20/80 × 35.20)	8.80
Target selling price	44.00

185 The maximum price that a profit-maximising company should be willing to pay to the outside supplier for the components is $40,000

If components are purchased outside:

	$
Contribution earned elsewhere	25,000
Variable cost saving	15,000
Maximum price to pay	40,000

186 D

When making a further processing decision it is necessary to consider incremental revenues and incremental costs. Apportionment of joint costs is NOT relevant to the decision.

187 D

A bad debt provision is an accounting entry and is not a cash flow. It is therefore not relevant for decision making. The other elements would all be relevant to the decision.

188 A

Full cost can include non-production as well as production costs so the first option is not true. The other options are all disadvantages of using full cost pricing.

189

	Relevant cost?
Accounting adjustments	
Incremental fixed costs	✓

Relevant costs are incremental, future, cash costs. Incremental fixed costs would therefore satisfy this definition. Accounting adjustments such as depreciation is not a cash cost and it would not satisfy this definition.

190 D

Opportunity costs are concerned with identifying the value of any benefit forgone as the result of choosing one course of action in preference to another. They will always be relevant for decision making purposes.

191

	Included?
Prime costs	✓
Direct labour supervision costs	
Variable sales distribution costs	✓
Depreciation on factory machinery	
Selling managers' salaries	

Only variable costs should be included when setting the selling price using marginal cost pricing.

192 The relevant cost of using the material is $460

As the material is not regularly used in the business the inventory should be used. This will be valued at the forgone revenue of $4 per kg, giving a value for the inventory of $160.

The remaining material needs to be purchased at a cost of $15 per kg, $300 in total.

This give a total relevant cost = $160 + $300 = $460.

193

	Correct?
Marginal cost-plus pricing should be only used for short term decision making.	✓
Cost-plus pricing requires that the profit mark-up applied by an organisation is fixed.	
Cost-plus pricing is a strategically focused approach, as it accounts for external factors.	
Full cost-plus pricing requires the budgeted level of output to be determined at the outset.	✓

Statement 1 is correct: Marginal or variable Cost-plus pricing is not suitable for long term pricing, as recovery of fixed cost may not be possible.

Statements 2 and 3 are not correct: Cost plus pricing is internally focused and a drawback of the technique is that it fails to consider external influence, like competitor pricing strategies.

The mark-up percentage does not have to be fixed: it can vary and be adjusted to reflect market conditions.

Statement 4 is correct: the budgeted level of output does need to be determined for full cost-plus pricing as it would be used to calculate the overhead absorption rate for the calculation of the full cost per unit.

194 The relevant cost of labour is $900

Existing staff are fully employed and cannot be used. The cost of the labour will be the cost of the agency work

= 20 × $45 = $900

195 B

This can be determined by recalculating the budgeted loss for the branch on a relevant cost basis:

	$000
Forgone revenue	(200)
Non-labour variable costs	150
Net labour saving	30
Relevant fixed costs	110
Net benefit of closure	90

The fixed costs should not include the allocated central costs as these will still be incurred even if the branch is closed down. But the rent charge should be included as this will be avoided if the branch is removed.

196 The net benefit from further processing Product Z is $6,000

The joint process costs are not relevant to the decision to further process. The further processing decision will increase revenue by $8,000 ($20 per unit) and will cost $2,000. The overall net benefit will therefore be $6,000.

197 C

Location A = (0.2 × 100) + (0.3 × 50) + (0.5 × 60) = 65

Location B = (0.2 × 70) + (0.3 × 60) + (0.5 × 70) = 67

Location C = (0.2 × 50) + (0.3 × 100) + (0.5 × 80) = 80

Location D = (0.2 × 40) + (0.3 × 70) + (0.5 × 100) = 79

198 D

	R	**S**	**T**
	$	$	$
Contribution per unit			
$(100 – 15 – 20 – 15)	50		
$(150 – 30 – 35 –20)		65	
$(160 – 25 – 30 – 22)			83
Direct labour cost per unit	20	35	30
Contribution per $1 of direct labour	2.50	1.85	2.77
Profitability ranking	2nd	3rd	1st

199

	Meal?
Most profitable	L
Least profitable	K

	K	**L**	**M**
Sales price	$5.00	$3.00	$4.40
Less variable costs	$3.60	$1.80	$3.15
Contribution per meal	$1.40	$1.20	$1.25
Minutes	÷ 10	÷ 4	÷ 8
Contribution per minute	$0.14	$0.30	$0.16

200 A

Marginal cost of production = \$9.00 + \$14.00 + \$6.00 = \$29.00

For a mark-up, the cost is always equal to 100% and so \$29.00 = 100%.

The selling price will be 125% of cost, which is \$29.00 × 1.25 = \$36.25.

\$38.67 was the selling price if a margin was used instead of a mark-up.

\$42.50 and \$45.33 were the selling prices if the mark-up/margin was calculated on full production cost and not the marginal production cost.

201 A, B, D, E

Options A, B and D are all qualitative aspects that should be taken into account when faced with such a decision. Although it is not always possible to place a numerical value to these factors, it is important that they are not ignored in the decision making process. Option E is an avoidable cost, which is also relevant.

Option C is not relevant.

BREAKEVEN ANALYSIS

202 B

$$\text{Breakeven sales revenue} = \frac{\text{fixed costs}}{\text{C/S ratio}}$$

$$800{,}000 = \frac{\$320{,}000}{\text{C/S ratio}}$$

$$\text{C/S ratio} = \frac{\$320{,}000}{\$800{,}000} = 40\%$$

Sales revenue required to achieve a target profit of \$50,000

$$= \frac{\$320{,}000 + \$50{,}000}{40\%} = \$925{,}000$$

203 C

Weighted average contribution to sales ratio:

$$\frac{(35\% \times 6) + (20\% \times 5) + (30\% \times 4)}{(6 + 5 + 4)}$$

$$= \frac{(210 + 100 + 120)\%}{15}$$

= 28.667%

Target contribution is obtained by adding back fixed costs to the target profit figure:

\$40,000 + \$160,000 = \$200,000.

Therefore, the sales required: 200,000/0.28667 = \$697,666 i.e. \$698,000 to the nearest \$1,000.

204 B

If the margin of safety budgeted in period 3 is 21.015%, then the breakeven number of units in the period is:

6,570 – (6,570 × 21.015%) = 5,189 units

At this level, contribution is equal to the level of fixed costs.

Contribution at this volume is:

5,189 × 35% × $72 = $130,763.

So fixed costs are $130,763 (which is nearest to B, i.e. $131,000).

205

	Required?
The product-specific fixed costs	✓
The product mix ratio	✓
General fixed costs	✓
The method of apportionment of general fixed costs	
Individual product gross contribution to sales ratios	✓

To calculate breakeven, we need total fixed costs (product-specific plus general fixed costs), the C/S ratio for each product and the product sales mix. The method of apportioning fixed costs is irrelevant.

206 A

First calculate the contribution to sales ratio for U:

S	60%	×	⅓	=	20.00%	
T	45%	×	⅓	=	15.00%	
U	51%	×	⅓	=	17.00%	(balancing figure)
Total				=	52.00%	

By changing the mix, the overall ratio becomes:

S	60%	×	45%	=	27.00%
T	45%	×	20%	=	9.00%
U	51%	×	35%	=	17.85%
Total				=	53.85%

207 B

The lowest breakeven sales revenue will be achieved if the products are sold in the order of the highest C/S ratio first, followed by the second highest and then the lowest. So the first thing we need to do is to identify which products have the highest C/S ratios.

	Product E	**Product F**	**Product G**
Sales revenue ($000)	1,200	1,500	1,900
Total contribution ($000)	360	300	475
C/S ratio	0.30	0.20	0.25
Rank	1st	3rd	2nd

To breakeven the total contribution must be $850,000 to cover the fixed costs.

The products with the two highest C/S ratios (Product E and G) have a combined total contribution of $835,000. Therefore, the remaining $15,000 contribution must come from Product F. Therefore, the revenue required from Product F = $15,000 / 0.20 = $75,000.

208 The margin of safety is 25.6%

Weighted average C/S ratio equals:

$$\frac{(3 \times 32\%)+(5 \times 48\%)}{3+5} = 42\%$$

$$\text{Breakeven point} = \frac{\text{fixed costs}}{\text{C/S ratio}} = \frac{\$200,000}{0.42} = \$476,190$$

Margin of safety = $640,000 – $476,190 = $163,810 or 25.6%

209 A

Weighted average contribution margin:

Product	**Sales mix**	**Contribution per contract**	**Weighted average contribution**
		$	$
Superior	20%	550	110
Standard	30%	500	150
Basic	50%	220	110
			370

$$\text{Breakeven point in units} = \frac{\$1,000,000}{\$370} = 2,703 \text{ contracts}$$

If these are sold in the proportion 20%:30%:50% then this gives sales of

Superior = 2,703 × 20% = 540.6

Standard = 2,703 × 30% = 810.9

Basic = 2,703 × 50% = 1,351.5

Multiplied by the sales revenue per contract gives total revenue of

(540.6 × $1,000) + (810.9 × $750) + (1,351.5 × $400) = $1,689,375

210 D

Contribution per unit \$14 – \$6	\$8
Breakeven point (BEP) = \$24,400 ÷ \$8	3,050 units
With new method:	
Contribution per unit \$15 – \$5	\$10
New fixed costs = \$24,400 × \$130%	\$31,720
BEP = \$31,720 ÷ \$10	3,172 units

BEP increases by 122 units

211 The monthly breakeven sales revenue is \$594,000

A weighted average contribution to sales (C/S) ratio needs to be calculated:

$$\frac{(3 \times 40\%) + (7 \times 30\%) + (5 \times 35\%)}{3+7+5} = 33.67\%$$

The monthly breakeven sales value is therefore the monthly fixed costs divided by the weighted average C/S ratio:

\$200,000/0.3367 = \$594,000

212 The minimum contribution that must be earned by a unit of product Y to make it worth producing units of product Y in a profit-maximising budget is \$4

Product Y uses more materials per unit than product X. If product X is manufactured, it will earn a contribution of \$6 per kilogram consumed and \$4 per labour hour. To make product Y worth making, it must earn at least the lower amount of \$6 per kilogram (\$24 per unit) or \$4 per labour hour (\$4 per unit). So the answer is \$4.

You could possibly work this out by drawing a linear programming graph: if the contribution per unit of Y exceeds \$24, the company will make Y only. If the contribution per unit of Y is less than \$4, it will make X only. If the contribution per unit of Y is over \$4 but less than \$24, the optimal production mix will be a combination of X and Y.

213 The margin of safety, expressed as a percentage of budgeted units is 25%

Budgeted contribution is \$8,000 + \$24,000 = \$32,000

Budgeted units are \$32,000 / \$10 per unit = 3,200 units

Breakeven point is \$24,000 ÷ \$10 = 2,400 units.

Margin of safety as a percentage is (3,200 units – 2,400 units) / 3,200 units = 25%

214 The breakeven sales revenue is \$120,000

Variable costs = 70% × \$50k = \$35k

Contribution = \$40k – \$35k = \$5k

Contribution to sales ratio = \$5k/\$40k = 12.5%

Fixed costs = 30% × \$50k = \$15k

Break even sales revenue = \$15k/12.5% = \$120k

215 The revenue that needs to be generated by Product Z for S plc to achieve the budgeted profit is $16 million

($10m × 0.15) + ($20m × 0.1) + ?m = $5.5m + $2m

$3.5m + ?m = $7.5m   so ? = $4m

Revenue needed to ensure a profit of $2m = 4/0.25 = $16m

216 D

The gradient of the line will decrease because the contribution per unit will be lower.

This will then mean that the breakeven point is achieved at a later point on the graph.

217 C

The P/V line will move down as profit will be lower at all units of sales. The gradient represents the C/S ratio and this will be unchanged.

218 A

The shaded area on the breakeven chart represents loss.

219 The budgeted profit is $160,000

The breakeven point is = $400,000/$20 = 20,000 units

$$\text{Margin of safety \%} = \frac{\text{margin of safety}}{\text{breakeven units}}$$

$$0.4 \text{ (or 40\%)} = \frac{\text{margin of safety}}{\text{20,000 units}}$$

Margin of safety = 0.4 × 20,000 units = 8,000 units

Expected profit = 8,000 units × $20 = $160,000

220 The breakeven sales revenue is $2,783,000

The weighted average contribution sales ratio can be determined:

$$\text{Weighted average c/s ratio} = \frac{\text{total contribution}}{\text{total revenue}} = \frac{(\$30 \times 50{,}000)+(\$40 \times 20{,}000)}{(\$40 \times 50{,}000)+(\$60 \times 20{,}000)}$$

= $2,300,000/$3,200,000

= 71.875%

The breakeven revenue = $2m/71.875% = $2,782,609

221 B

If products are sold in the order of the most favourable contribution to sales ratio, the upper line on the diagram would represent the expected total sales revenue. The point at which it cuts the horizontal axis would represent the break-even point. This is closest to $400,000.

222 B

Assuming products are sold in order of their contribution to sales ratio can help create the profit volume chart, but it is not necessary to assume this when determining the break-even point.

The other statements are valid assumptions of the technique.

223 The breakeven sales revenue is $29,000

The weighted average contribution per unit = (70% × 75%) + (30% × 80%) = 76.5%

The breakeven sales revenue = $22,000/76.5% = $28,758

224 B

Break even volume = 7,200 – (7,200 × 26.2%) = 5,314 units

Contribution at break-even point = Fixed costs

Contribution at break-even point = 5,314 × 21% × $56 = $62,493 = Fixed costs

225 B

Point A represents variable costs. It is the difference between the total cost line and the fixed cost line.

226 B, C

Statement B is correct. If the fixed costs remain the same, but more customers are purchasing the product with a lower C/S ratio, then the weighted average contribution will reduce, increasing the breakeven point. If the total expected volume of sales is not expected to change, then the margin of safety will reduce.

Statement C is correct. The starting point of the line is at the value of fixed costs. We are told that the cost estimates are expected to stay the same and so the fixed costs will be the same. The starting point of the line on the y axis will therefore be in the same place.

Statement A is incorrect. The gradient of the line represents the weighted average contribution per unit. If customers are switching from Product Z to Product Z then this means that a larger proportion of customers will be purchasing a product with a lower C/S ratio, which will result in a lower weighted average contribution per unit.

Statement D is incorrect. The breakeven point will increase due to the reduction in the weighted average contribution per unit.

LINEAR PROGRAMMING

227 The shadow price per litre for material is $1

The original contribution is = (4 × 400) + (2 × 600) = $2,800

The revised contribution is = (4 × 400.5) + (2 × 599.5) = $2,801

The shadow price for materials = 2,801 – 2,800 = $1 per litre

228 B

Linear programming assumes that products are infinitely divisible and that parts of units can be produced and sold.

The other statements are true.

229 D

If, say, X = 400, Y would = 800. The only equation that satisfies these numbers is the correct answer.

230 The highest acceptable price per kg for extra material is $6

This will be the normal price, $4 per kg, plus the shadow price, $2 per kg.

231 B

The optimal production plan will have to be determined by using a simultaneous equations technique.

If the Material X function is multiplied by 3:

Material X: 3A + 6B = 27,000

Material Y: 3A + B = 12,000

Deducting one from the other, leaves:

5B = 15,000

B = 3,000

Substituting this into one of the equations:

3A + (1 × 3,000) = 12,000

3A = 9,000

A = 3,000

232 A

Each unit of A (X) requires 5 hours of unskilled labour so the equation must contain 5X. Each unit of B (Y) requires 1 hour of unskilled labour so the equation must contain 1Y.

233 C

A shadow price for a scarce resource is its opportunity cost. It is the amount of contribution that would be lost if one unit less of that resource were available. It is similarly the amount of additional contribution that would be earned if one unit more of that resource were available. (This is on the assumption that the scarce resource is available at its normal variable cost.)

234 D

The company maximises contribution by producing B. Contribution per unit of material is:

$\frac{\$8.50}{2.5\text{kg}}$ = \$3.40 and this is the shadow price.

235 The maximum contribution which can be earned from these two products is \$8,250.

Simultaneous equations can be used to identify the optimum number of Product X and Product Y. However, firstly we must adjust one of the formula so that part of the equations is the same. This can be done by doubling equation for materials to $4X + 12Y \leq 3,400$.

Next compare the adjusted materials formula with the formula for machine hours.

Materials (adjusted): $4X + 12Y \leq 3,400$

Machine hours: $4X + 8Y \leq 2,500$

The difference is that the top formula has an additional 4Y and an additional 900.

So if 4Y = 900, Y will be equal to 900 / 4 = 225 units.

If Y = 225 then 4X + (12 × 225 units) = 3,400.

4X = 3,400 – (12 × 225 units)

4X = 700

X = 175

Total contribution = (\$15 per unit × 175 units) + (\$25 per unit × 225 units) = \$8,250.

236 The number of spare machine hours available (slack) will be 175 hours.

The optimum number of Product X and Product Y can be calculated as follows:

Materials $4X + 6Y \leq 2,000$

Labour: $4X + 8Y \leq 2,500$

The difference is that the bottom formula has an additional 2Y and an additional 500.

So if 2Y = 500, Y will be equal to 500 / 2 = 250 units.

If Y = 250 then 4X + (6 × 250 units) = 2,000.

4X = 2,000 – (6 × 250 units)

4X = 500

X = 125

Total machine hours required is (3 × 125 units) + (5 × 250 units) = 1,625 hours.

Spare hours available will be 1,800 hours – 1,625 hours = 175 hours.

237

	Shadow price > 0?
Direct labour hours	✓
Material A	
Material B	
Machine hours	

Only resources that meet at the optimal point will have a shadow price. This is at point B, where the direct labour line meets line R. The other constraints lines are above this point and there therefore must be slack in these resources which could be put to other uses. Resources that have a slack do not have a shadow price.

238

	Limitation?
Linear relationships must exist	✓
There can only be two products	✓
There can only be two scarce resources	
All variables must be completely divisible	✓
A computer must be used to find the optimal point	

Linear programming can cope with any number of constraints and the solution does not always need to be solved by a computer.

239 B

This should be based on contribution per unit:

Product	**J**	**L**
	$/unit	$/unit
Selling price	115	120
Direct material A ($10 per kg)	20	10
Direct material B ($6 per kg)	12	24
Skilled labour ($14 per hour)	28	21
Variable overhead ($4 per machine hour)	14	18
Contribution	41	47

And the iso-contribution line is 41J + 47L = M

240 The number of units of Product Y produced in order to maximise contribution (to the nearest whole unit) is 8,000 units.

The optimal production plan will have to be determined by using a simultaneous equations technique.

If the unskilled labour function is multiplied by 3:

Skilled labour: $6X + 4Y \leq 62,000$

Unskilled labour: $6X + 15Y \leq 150,000$

Deducting one from the other, leaves:

$11Y = 88,000$

$Y = 8,000$

241 The maximum amount of Material A available is 2,000 kgs

The line crosses the horizontal axis at coordinates T = 0 and R = 1,000. If each unit of R takes 2 kgs of Material A, then there must be 2,000 kgs of Material A available.

242 C

The optimal production plan will have to be determined by using a simultaneous equations technique.

If the Material X function is multiplied by 2:

Material X: $2A + 4B = 16,000$

Material Y: $2A + B = 13,000$

Deducting one from the other, leaves:

$3B = 3,000$

$B = 1,000$

Substituting this into one of the equations:

$2A + (4 \times 1,000) = 16,000$

$2A = 12,000$

$A = 6,000$

243 The maximum number of units of Product B which can be produced is 60 units.

If all of the resources have less than or equal to constraints, then the feasible region cannot exceed the lowest of the lines on the diagram. This means that the maximum number of units of Product B that can be produced can be no higher than where this line meets the vertical axis which is at 60 units.

244 B, C

Statements B and C are correct.

Statement A is incorrect. Linear programming can be used for profit maximisation or cost minimisation problems.

Statement D is incorrect. One of the limitations of linear programming is that it is only suitable when there is one clearly defined objective function.

245 B

All statements are said to be advantages of spreadsheet software with the exception of statement (i). Spreadsheets can not identify data input errors, apart from obvious errors such as inputting a letter instead of number, and therefore the analysis they prove can still be incorrect if the initial data is not inputted accurately.

RISK AND UNCERTAINTY IN THE SHORT TERM

RISK AND UNCERTAINTY IN THE SHORT TERM

246 If orders must be placed before the daily demand is known, the number of units that should be purchased at the beginning of each day in order to maximise expected profit is 200 units

Produce a payoff table:

Demand	**Probability**		**Supply**	
		100	200	300
100 units	0.25	$400	$0 (W1)	($400) (W2)
200 units	0.40	$400	$800	$400 (W3)
300 units	0.35	$400	$800	$1,200

Workings

(W1)	(100 × $8) – (200 × $4)	=	$0
(W2)	(100 × $8) – (300 × $4)	=	($400)
(W3)	(200 × $8) – (300 × $4)	=	$400

Expected profits:

If supply 100 units, EVs	=	$400
If supply 200 units, EV = ($0 × 0.25) + ($800 × 0.4) + ($800 × 0.35)	=	$600
If supply 300 units, EV = (($400) × 0.25) + ($400 × 0.4) + ($1,200 × 0.35)	=	$480

Therefore, profit is maximised by supplying 200 units.

247 The probability that the weekly contribution will exceed $20,000 is 45%

To generate a contribution greater than $20,000 it is necessary to earn a unit contribution greater than $20. Consider each of the feasible combinations:

Selling price	Variable cost	Contribution	Probability
$	$	$	
50	20	30	0.45 × 0.55 = 0.2475
60	20	40	0.25 × 0.55 = 0.1375
60	30	30	0.25 × 0.25 = 0.0625
		Answer =	**0.4475**

Answer = 44.75% = 45% to nearest full %

248 B

Project	**EV**	**Workings**
	$000	
L	500	(500 × 0.2) + (470 × 0.5) + (550 × 0.3)
M	526	(400 × 0.2) + (550 × 0.5) + (570 × 0.3)
N	432.5	(450 × 0.2) + (400 × 0.5) + (475 × 0.3)
O	398	etc.
P	497.5	

Therefore, Project M will maximise expected cash.

249 Assuming the baker adopts the minimax regret decision rule, the number of batches of bread that he/she/they should bake each day is 12 batches

Regret table		**Batches baked**		
		10	11	12
	10	0	20	40
Daily demand	11	50	0	20
	12	100	50	0
Max. regret		100	50	40

So to minimise the maximum regret the baker should bake 12 batches.

250

Decision criteria	Attitude to risk
Expected values	Risk neutral
Maximax	Risk seeker
Maximin	Risk averse
Minimax regret	Risk averse

251 A

The expected value is

= −2m + [(0.8 × 9.2m) + (0.2 × −1m)] = $5.16m

252 The probability that the variance is less than $45,000 is 0.13%

The mean is $60,000. $45,000 is $15,000 away from the mean.

This represents $15,000/$5,000 = 3.00 standard deviations. This is the z score.

From tables, on the left hand column, look up the z score to one decimal place, i.e. 3.0. Look along this row until it meets the column with the 2nd decimal place (0.00). The table gives us 0.4987.

This means that when looking at the 50% of variances that are below the mean 49.87% of them are within 3 standard deviations. Therefore, the probability that the variance will be below $45,000 is the remaining 0.13%

253 B

Minimax regret table:

	Order level			
Demand	**20 bunches**	**30 bunches**	**40 bunches**	**50 bunches**
20 bunches	$0	$40 **	$80	$120
30 bunches	$30	$0	$40	$80
40 bunches	$60	$30	$0	$40
50 bunches	$90	$60	$30	$0

** Working:

If demand is 20 bunches, the optimum order level would have been 20 bunches. In this situation a profit of $60 would have been made (as per payoff table). This is the maximum profit available for a demand of 20.

If the florist had ordered 30 bunches instead of 20 then he/she/they would have ordered too many and would have made a profit of just $20, therefore the value of the regret is the difference between the optimum profit and the actual profit. In this case the regret would be $60 – $20 = $40.

The maximum regret for 20 bunches is $90

The maximum regret for 30 bunches is $60

The maximum regret for 40 bunches is $80

The maximum regret for 50 bunches is $120

If the florist wishes to minimise the maximum regret 30 bunches should be ordered.

254 A

The value of perfect information =

Expected profit with the information – expected profit without the information.

In this scenario the value of the perfect information is $15,000.

The expected profit without the information is $142,000.

Therefor the expected profit with the information is $142,000 + $15,000 = $157,000

255 A

Perfect information is always 100% accurate. By comparison imperfect information is usually correct but can be incorrect.

256 The probability that lowering the selling price to $45 per unit would increase profit is 82%

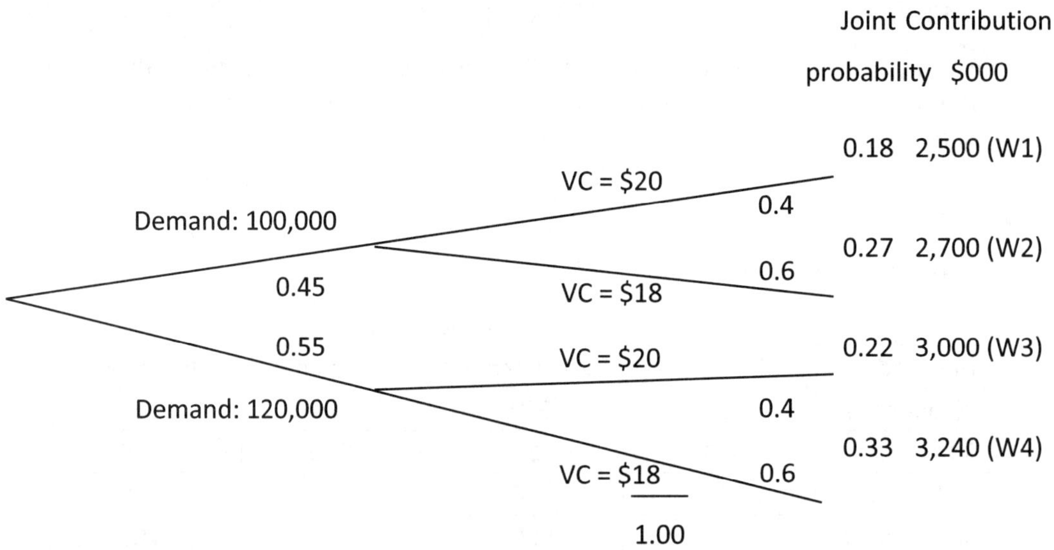

Existing contribution = ($50 – $21) × 90,000 units = 2,610 ($000)

Contribution is greater than this in (W2), (W3) and (W4) above.

∴ The probability of the profit being higher is = 0.27 + 0.22 + 0.33 = 0.82

Workings

(W1) ($45 – $20) × 100,000 units

(W2) ($45 – $18) × 100,000 units

(W3) ($45 – $20) × 120,000 units

(W4) ($45 – $18) × 120,000 units

257 D

Expected selling price		**Expected cost**	
	$		$
\$20 × 0.25	5	\$8 × 0.2	1.6
\$25 × 0.4	10	\$10 × 0.5	5
\$30 × 0.35	10.5	\$12 × 0.3	3.6
	25.5		10.2

Expected unit contribution = \$25.50 – \$10.20 = \$15.30 × 1,000 = \$15,300

258 Which of the following are disadvantages of using an expected value technique?

	Disadvantage of EVs?
Expected values only provides the most likely result	
It ignores attitudes to risk	✓
Only two possible outcomes can be considered	
Probabilities are subjective	✓
The answer provided may not exist	✓

259 B

The minimum outcome for a fee of \$600 is \$360k

The minimum outcome for a fee of \$800 is \$400k

The minimum outcome for a fee of \$900 is \$360k

The minimum outcome for a fee of \$1,000 is \$320k

Therefore, if the committee wants to maximise the minimum cash inflow it will set a fee of \$800.

260 The number of cakes that should be baked if the maximax decision criterion is applied is 30.

If the maximax decision criterion is applied, then the café owner would bake 30 cakes each day as the maximum contribution of \$21 is to be gained at this level.

261 D

If market condition is forecast as Poor, then Project P should be chosen as this project yields the highest cash flow under a poor market.

However, if the market condition is forecast as Good or Excellent, then Project M should be chosen as M will yield the highest cash.

In summary:

Market condition	**Selected project**	**Cash (x)** $000	**Probability (p)**	**px**
Poor	P	600	0.20	120
Good	M	550	0.50	275
Excellent	M	570	0.30	171
			1.00	566

Expected return with perfect information	$566,000
Expected return without (Project M)	$526,000
∴ Value of information	$40,000

262 B

The maximum regret for product W is $43,000

The maximum regret for product X is $17,000

The maximum regret for product Y is $73,000

The maximum regret for product Z is $38,000

263 B

Point G represents a decision point. If the decision is taken to licence, then there is a value of $6m.

The other decision is to further invest – which appears to have a cost of $4m. But this then opens up the chance point where there is a 70% chance of making $22m and a 30% chance of making $9m. So this decision to further invest would have an expected value of:

= –4m + [(0.7 × 22) + (0.3 × 9)] = $14.1m

Therefore, the decision to further invest is worth more than the licencing option. The company would choose to invest and would make $14.1m.

264 The maximum amount that should be paid for the information from the market research company is $7,500.

The value of perfect information is calculated as:

Expected value with perfect information – Expected value without perfect information.

Expected value without perfect information:

The expected value without perfect information is $880,000.

Expected value with perfect information:

Demand	**Sales price**	**Profit (x)**	**Prob (p)**	**px**
High	$105	$1,725,000	30%	$517,500
Medium	$100	$700,000	50%	$350,000
Low	$100	$100,000	20%	$20,000
			EV	**$887,500**

The value of perfect information is $887,500 – $880,000 = $7,500

265 C

The information provided by the meteorologist is called imperfect information. The value of imperfect information is calculated in the same way as the value of perfect information:

Expected profit with the information – expected profit without the information.

In this scenario we already know the value of the information: S Ltd is prepared to pay $30,000 for the information.

We have also been told that the expected profit with the information is $1,250,000.

We therefore have to calculate the expected profit without the information:

= $1,250,000 – $30,000 = $1,220,000

266 The maximum amount that should be paid for the information from the market research company is $11,440.

The value of perfect information is calculated as:

Expected value with perfect information – Expected value without perfect information.

Expected value without perfect information:

The expected value without perfect information is $719,700.

Expected value with perfect information:

Demand	**Shop size**	**Profit (x)**	**Prob (p)**	**px**
Strong	LARGE	1,413,200	0.2	282,640
Good	LARGE	865,700	0.4	346,280
Weak	MEDIUM	255,550	0.4	102,220
			Expected value	731,140

The value of perfect information is $731,140 – $719,700 = $11,440

267 The number of cakes that should be baked if the maximin decision criterion is applied is 20.

	Number of cakes baked		
	20	25	30
Worst contribution	$14	$11.5	$9

If 20 cakes are baked the worst contribution would be $14, this is the best "worst contribution"

268 A

A regret matrix is shown below:

	Membership level		
Membership fee	**Low** $000	**Average** $000	**High** $000
$600	40	0	0
$800	0	40	60
$900	40	75	45
$1,000	80	100	120

Maximum regret if set fee of $600 is $40k

Maximum regret if set fee of $800 is $60k

Maximum regret if set fee of $900 is $75k

Maximum regret if set fee of $1,000 is $120k

To minimise the maximum regret a fee of $600 should be set.

269 The expected value of the company profit if the selling price is reduced to $45 per unit is $1,708,200

Expected demand:	
(100,000 × 0.45) + (120,000 × 0.55)	111,000 units
Expected variable cost:	
($20 × 0.40) + ($18 × 0.60)	$18.80
Contribution per unit:	
$45 – $18.80	$26.20
Expected contribution:	
111,000 × $26.20	$2,908,200
Less fixed costs	($1,200,000)
Expected profit	$1,708,200

270 The expected value at point A on the decision trees (to the nearest $0.1m) is $22m

Point A represents a decision point. If the decision is taken to outsource then there is a value of $22m.

The other decision is to further invest – which appears to have a cost of $20m. But this then opens up the chance point where there is a 60% chance of making $60m and a 40% chance of making $12m. So this decision to further invest would have an expected value of:

= –20m + [(0.6 × 60) + (0.4 × 12)] = $20.8m

Therefore, the decision to further invest is worth less than the outsourcing option. The company would choose to outsource and would make $22m.

271 C

Monthly contribution will exceed $13,500 if unit contribution exceeds $13.50. This will be the case for the following combinations:

Sales price	Variable cost	Unit contribution	Probability	Joint probability
$25	($8)	$17	0.4 × 0.2	0.08
$25	($10)	$15	0.4 × 0.5	0.20
$30	($8)	$22		
$30	($10)	$20	0.35 × 1	0.35
$30	($12)	$18		
Total				0.63

272 Using expected values, the financial benefit from hiring the orchestra for the concert is $915

The expected audience size = (0.5 × 300) + (0.3 × 400) + (0.2 × 500) = 370

The expected contribution = 370 × [(0.7 × 25) + (0.3 × 40)] = $10,915

The financial benefit from hiring the orchestra is $10,915 – $10,000 = $915

Therefore, it is worthwhile hiring the orchestra for the concert.

273

	True?
As standard deviation increases risk increases	✓
Imperfect information cannot be 100% correct	
A risk seeking investor typically focuses on expected values	
Expected value calculations consider the range of possible outcomes	
A variable with a smaller coefficient of variation is less risky	✓

Imperfect information is sometimes correct, but can also be incorrect. Whilst perfect information is always 100% correct.

Risk seeking investors are likely to select the strategy with the best possible outcomes, regardless of the likelihood that they will occur. These decision makers will ignore the expected value.

Expected values ignore the range of possible outcomes. The other statements are true.

274 D

The original expected value will be calculated as EV = (\$24,000 × 0.7) + ((\$8,000) × 0.3) = \$14,400. This suggests that the delivery service should be launched.

The EV would have to decrease by \$14,400 before the original decision is reversed.

Let the level of the loss be 'L'

Currently, EV = (24 × 0.7) + (L × 0.3) = 16.8 + 0.3L

If EV falls to zero:

0 = 16.8 + 0.3L

0.3L = -16.8

L = -16.8/0.3 = -56

The loss would have to increase from \$8,000 to \$56,000 before the decision is reversed. This is an increase of \$48,000/\$8,000 × 100% = 600%.

275 D

Best and worst outcomes are not classified attitudes to risk

Risk neutral decision makers would use expected values to make their decisions.

Risk averse decision makers would choose the project with the most likely outcome.

276 C

The expected value is an amalgamation of several possible outcomes and their associated probabilities so it may not correspond to any of the actual possible outcomes. So statement (i) is incorrect.

The expected value takes risk into account as it considers the probability of each outcome. Therefore, statement (ii) is correct.

The expected value does not give an indication of the dispersion of the possible outcomes; a standard deviation would be needed for this. Therefore, statement (iii) is correct.

The EV is merely a weighted average and therefore has little meaning for a one-off project. Therefore, statement (iv) is incorrect.

277 The individual is risk averse and so will look to invest in the least risky project, which is project 3. This is the one with the smallest coefficient of variation. The coefficient of variation is found by dividing the standard deviation by the EV.

Project	**EV of return \$**	**Standard deviation**	**Coefficient of variation**
1	4,300	550	12.8%
2	1,800	380	21.1%
3	6,300	600	9.5%